DREAMS AS THE GATEWAY TO THE DEITY

(Based on thousands of the author's own dreams)

M. Saleh Abusaidi, Ph.D

iUniverse LLC
Bloomington

DREAMS AS THE GATEWAY TO THE DEITY
(BASED ON THOUSANDS OF THE AUTHOR'S OWN DREAMS)

iUniverse books may be ordered through booksellers or by contacting:

iUniverse LLC
1663 Liberty Drive
Bloomington, IN 47403
www.iuniverse.com
1-800-Authors (1-800-288-4677)

ISBN: 978-1-4759-9313-4 (sc)
ISBN: 978-1-4759-9314-1 (e)

Library of Congress Control Number: 2013912635

Printed in the United States of America.

iUniverse rev. date: 02/27/2014

To all of those people who see themselves as one with the Creator.

Acknowledgements

I AM ESPECIALLY grateful to two good friends, Larry Luta and Bonnie Soto, who read the manuscript at various stages and helped not only with editing but giving me full encouragement. My deepest appreciation is extended to Professor Arthur T. Jersild, who during my studies at Columbia University, introduced me to the field of self-psychology. I also wish to express my thanks to Danile Wilson, my assistant. The preparation of the manuscript was significantly facilitated by her skill in producing a readable copy from a very rough draft.

True Books

... A BOOK is written, not to multiply the voice merely, not to carry it merely, but to perpetuate it. The author has something to say which he perceives to be true and useful, or helpfully beautiful. So far as he knows no one has yet said it; so far as he knows, no one else can say it. He is bound to say it, clearly and melodiously if he may; clearly at all events. In the sum of his life he finds this to be the thing, or group of things, manifest to him;-this, the piece of true knowledge, or sight which his share of sunshine and earth has permitted him to seize. He would fain set it down forever; engrave it on rock, if he could; saying, "This is the best of me; for the rest, I ate, and drank, and slept, loved, and hated, like another; my life was as the vapor, and is not; but this I saw and knew; this, if anything of mine, is worth your memory." That is his 'writing'; it is, in his small human way, and with whatever degree of true inspiration is in him, his inscription, or scripture. That is a 'Book.'

John Ruskin in A Treasury of Philosophy

Table of Contents

Introduction

THIS BOOK IS a detailed account of the meaning and purpose of dreams based on my lifetime involvement with a very large number of dreams of my own. For nearly four decades, I have had numerous dreams every night. I have noted them in bed as soon as they occurred and rewrote them in the morning. The number of such dream journals currently adds up to 255 volumes. What I have learned from these voluminous dreams has been highly inspiring as well as spiritually enlightening. I have gained some knowledge that I believe to be both true and also rather new. Since no one else can say what I have learned from this unique experience, I set it down in this book for others to see and to compare with their own dreams and worldviews.

A legitimate question that most of us have is: why do we dream? A short answer is that we dream to learn what is real, what is unreal, what is worth pursuing, and what is best avoiding. In other words, dreams reveal reality. To know what is real is of vital and fundamental importance. A life lived in illusion or a phantom-like state is not worth living. I believe nothing so much can convince us of the nature of reality as can our dreams. The problem with our dreams, as shall been seen later, is their cryptic nature. Almost all dreams are enigmatic, shadowy, and vague. However, once we become interested in them and follow them closely and long enough, we find as much consistency, meaningfulness and clarity as we would find in scientific methods.

The dreams I have recorded are of two kinds: long, narrative, visual dreams and short, verbal, auditory dreams. Dreams quoted in this book are of the latter kind. Generally, they consist of a curt statement. As such they are not representative of some tens of thousands of the longer dreams that I have had but are not included here because they would need pages of explanation. The short dreams have been cited mainly because they are largely straightforward verbatim messages and because a good portion of them were delivered in English. However, a substantial number of dreams quoted had to be translated or extrapolated from Persian, as Persian is my mother tongue. Although some dreams have been interpreted broadly, every effort has been made not to alter or distort the literal meaning. Deciphering and figuring out the meaning of each dream has been an arduous and perplexing task, but the satisfaction obtained from solving the puzzle involved in each case made the effort not only worthwhile but highly enlightening.

According to these dreams (a small portion of which are included in this book and henceforth will be referred to as "received dreams"), almost all of us have vicarious or inexperienced concepts of reality. What we know about reality is acquired through sympathetic participation in the belief system of significant others around us. If their beliefs are spurious what we learn from them will be spurious too. Our dreams discredit this concept of reality. The kind of reality that our dreams expose is experiential; it must be derived from our own experience. What we believe to be real or unreal, true or untrue should not be based on the words others have expressed to us, unless such words agree with our first-hand experiences.

How can concepts that are vague and shadowy be explained at all? We need to go beyond the ordinary, the obvious and the common limits of knowledge and perception. The world of dreams transports us beyond the ordinary, and makes us see and experience things beyond those wildest imaginable. While in a dream state, we have no awareness; yet after waking, there is no doubt that what we underwent in that sleep state was fact and was our own experience. In this manner, dreaming provides our daytime reality with solid ground.

A number of short dreams have been quoted here in support of what I have extrapolated from each topic. I have deliberately included many relevant dreams in the hope that the picture of reality that dreams present to us may become clear. Some readers by reviewing what is presented may detect additional meanings beyond those presented; if that happens certainly the enormity of the quotation will not be in vain. What needs to be kept in mind is that I have not fabricated or altered any of the quotes. However, the introductory remarks in each section are my commentary and are mainly interpretative or an enlargement of ideas expressed by the received dream. The aim has been to better convey the meaning of the dreams rather than by expressing my own views.

The reality that our dreams bring to light relates to three domains: 1) the reality of human identity; 2) the reality of the deity; and 3) the reality of the relationship between the two. The aforementioned themes constitute the content of this work. What needs to be added here is that topics discussed in this book have been considered by theologians, philosophers, mystics and various Eastern traditions in almost all ages. Reference to the views of some of the thinkers in these fields has been made to enhance understanding of the material presented by the dreams. However, at least in one respect what is set forth here is different from all that has been said by others, namely, the source of presentation here has been all dreams, not speculation.

The quest for the meaning of dreams is certainly one of the major endeavors in human history. Topics such as dreams, self, or consciousness have been considered as questions—begging issues in modern psychology. Hence, discussions have been abandoned as it is believed that dreams do not lend themselves to scientific methods of analysis. However, based on my experience, dreams can also be subjected to the same rigorous method of investigation as other areas of scientific inquiry. What we need to do is to look for repetition, coherence, and internal consistency. I believe dreams are an important source of knowledge and an excellent vehicle for seeing a deeper level of reality. As such, they should be studied more carefully. Perhaps nothing can show us more of the boundlessness of the phenomenon of self than its operation in dreaming.

I make no claims to have understood all of my dreams thoroughly, and I have no illusion of infallibility. It is always extremely difficult to be precise and clear about metaphysical issues. However, the dreams quoted are largely verbatim messages. If some messages are found vague, probably the aim is that some mysteries must always remain such to keep the field of inquiry open. It should also be noted that formal nomenclature or pedantic philosophical jargon was avoided. It is my hope that the dreams quoted will serve as a fountainhead of inspiration and awakening.

Chapter 1

Why Do We Dream?

Dreams are made of divine substance.

~Plotinus

*When the topsy turveyness of dreams are grasped
then we understand plainest truth.*

~D.T. Suzuki

HUMAN BEINGS OF all ages have been interested in their dreams as well as have been puzzled by them. Few other human experiences seem to have aroused so much befuddlement and so much speculation as dreams and their meanings. The enormity of writings and books on this topic since antiquity testifies to the depth of the dreamers' interest in understanding this phenomenon. Moreover, all of us have had some dreams at one time or another that have visited us involuntarily. Unless we resort to very strong drugs, we have no defense against them.

A good many questions have arisen in our minds regarding these nocturnal experiences. We want to know why we dream, what causes dreams, what is their source, and why are they so enigmatic? Why do these particular persons, objects, or frightening events appear in our dreams? Are our dreams telling us something about the future? Are they meaningful or meaningless? In short, do they serve a purpose, or are they chance events or unsolicited guests? No one thus far has provided satisfactory answers to these questions. The human thirst for finding answers to these questions harks back to the dawn of history. In effect, some authorities even believe

1

that the interest of the ancients in remembering their dreams led them to recount their experience in some forms of signs and symbols, and such attempts eventually evolved into common script.

Of all the questions posed above, perhaps the most important is whether dreams are purposeful—intended to serve a useful end. According to the received dreams a short answer to this is a positive yes. The fact that dreams are universal and spontaneous indicates that like all other spontaneous functions in our bodies, they are not aimless or meaningless. Without our awareness and without any effort on our part, our heart pumps blood through our arteries, our lungs supply our blood with oxygen, and our glands secrete substances the body needs. All these systems and many, many more operate independently and autonomously to keep us healthy and alive. There must also be some purpose for the events of dreaming that occur spontaneously without our control. We ask ourselves: Why do we have a dream and what does it tell us? Briefly, we dream to become disillusioned and learn of reality that is beyond the reach of intelligence.

Based on forty years of study, analysis, and involvement with my own dreams, I can state with a high degree of confidence that the purpose of dreams is to correct our misperceptions and reveal to us what is reality as a matter of fact. As noted in the introduction the reality that our dreams uncover relates to the genuine human identity or the self, to true knowledge of the nature of the Divine, and to one's life purpose and meaning.

What is meant by a dream? How can we define it? Based on my comprehension, dreams are messages from an omniscient source who knows intimately the details of every dreamer's life and accordingly composes a dream that is tailor-made to the circumstances of the dreamer in a way that the message eventually may lead that dreamer to gain an insight into reality. This source seems to be omniscient as it has first-hand knowledge concerning the language that various dreamers speak, their strivings and frustrations, their friends and foes, the places they have lived, the experiences they have gained, the setbacks and triumphs they have had and their hopes, desires and expectations.

Freud's theory of dreams is that dreams are wish fulfillment. For example, if you have an unsatisfied sexual urge, you will have a sexual dream. He and his followers claimed that dreams are excited by such sources as the dreamer's childhood memories, memories of the day's events, past experiences, immediate sleep environment, and their psychological states. I believe subsuming dreams that are cognitive under mechanical laws, flies in the face of common sense. Physical conditions or psychological states are devoid of the ability to produce dreams or to design intricate scenarios and narratives with profound meaning. The stomach and brainstem are unconscious, they cannot think. Dreams are subject to the processes of logical thought. They are beyond the realm of the unthinking matter.

Recent trends in dream research have come up with conclusions that fare no better than the work of predecessors. They assert that we sleep to give the brain time to dream; that the cell groups in the brainstem incite the content of dreams; that dreams are the garbage disposal of the mind; that, while dreaming, useless information that interferes with rational thought is flushed away; that dreams are not only meaningless but also harmful if retained in our memory, hence they should be forgotten; that dream processes are actually close to ordinary waking processes; and that dreams are simpler, less mysterious, and more down-to-earth than they are often thought to be. However, none of the researchers who have made the above assertions have been able to support their claims with sufficient data.

In contrast with what was just mentioned above, my dreams reveal that they are generally more real and more meaningful than our waking concept of reality. In a sense, they are a shortcut to the truths; they are intended to enlighten us about the nature of reality. However, for reasons that will be discussed later, they are largely shrouded in symbolic language. The point to keep in mind is that social norms and order as well as cultural traditions and organizations have a life of their own. Social change does occur at a superficial level but rarely at a deeper level. The mysteries and superstitions that surround the thought of almost everyone in all societies are inveterate. On the whole, they are enduring and unremitting. Nonetheless, dreams challenge such institutions as well as traditional social customs and beliefs. In a way, dreams are iconoclasts. They attack settled beliefs and show us what is right, true, or real. Without dream meditation, the prospect for real change and progress is rather scant.

How to Understand Dreams

To understand dreams, we need to become knowledgeable in at least three areas:

1. The dream's themes (or what they are talking about)
2. The dream's symbolic language
3. The dream's methods of guidance

The Dream's Theme

Dreams use countless figures, images, and symbols to convey their messages. They use persons such as father, mother, relative, children, bosses, colleagues, classmates, friends, enemies, ad infinitum. They show location where one has been or one currently lives, such as houses, schools, stadium, kitchen, living room, bedrooms. They set up pleasant natural scenery, such as fields, valleys, mountains, rivers, lakes, oceans, or unpleasant, scary settings or surroundings such as precipices, ridges, cliffs, canyons, ravines. Also frequently, dreams contain animals or creatures that are pretty and friendly such as birds, pets, and lambs, or ferocious, ugly and unfriendly such as lions or snakes or other dangerous animals. Dreams also present us with a plethora of objects such as cars, bicycles, boats, and planes; or events such as a ringing telephone, driving, flying, playing, climbing, love-making, fighting or being robbed, being attacked by incubus, having a car accident, experiencing an earthquake, explosion, death and dying.

Hardly any of the above elements and events express or are representative of what their names denote. Father does not refer to the father we know of. Boat has nothing to do with the one we use on the water. Climbing does not refer to the activity of going up a mountain, dying does not signify that someone will pass away. These and many more only speak for three central themes of the dreams, namely:

1. Who we are, what we do with our lives and who we should be;
2. The nature of the Divine and how we can know Him; and
3. Our lives' tasks and ends

Thus the array of figures and images in our dreams stands for or suggests something other than that with which we are familiar. They all

4

carry ideas or meanings that ultimately should lead us to the understanding of the true identity of the human and the Divine, as well as of the purpose of human life.

Of course this does not always mean our dreams will be symbolic and cryptic. Gradually dream messages should become less puzzling and more and more clear. In my case, during the last ten years most of the dreams were plain or literal, adhering largely to the ordinary or primary meaning of the terms used in everyday language. This is evidenced by the dreams to be quoted in various parts of this book.

The Dream's Symbolic Language

Understanding a dream requires understanding symbolic language as indicated above. Principally a symbol in a dream is a vehicle through which sacred concepts can be transmitted. The symbol can be a picture, a word, an event, an emotional state, a letter of the alphabet, a syllable, or a figure. No matter what form symbols take, they convey an idea or thought pertaining to the three central themes of the dream. So long as we do not know what our symbols suggest, our dreams remain vague or inscrutable. Some authors hold that there are universal symbols that mean the same thing in everyone's dreams. Based on my experience, symbols are personal. They are geared to the particular life situation of each dreamer.

In my dreams, symbols gradually became intelligible through guidance from the dream itself. I discovered that the bulk of my dreams are composed of rebuses and puns. A rebus is a presentation of words or syllables by picture, whose names resemble the intended words or syllable only in sound. For example, the word "although" may stand for all (is) thou, or seeing someone in the dream whose name is Walter Myhoff, probably has nothing to do with the friend we know by that particular name. The dream is concerned with what the syllables of the name of this person can convey. In this case, it could stand for "double you" (and) "alter (are) my half." In this method of communication, the sound of syllables or vocable is important, not the actual spelling or conventional meaning. Thus the names of each image in the dream when split into sub-units should convey a message consistent with the overall teachings of dreams. When dreams are regarded as rebuses, their bizarre and puzzling character will fall away. Another difficulty in understanding dreams is the use of polysemous terms rather than univocal words. The dreamer must guess which meaning is applicable.

An additional problem, in the way of comprehending dreams, is the use of the familiar incident of recent time or people about whom we were concerned within the past few days. The immediate response of the person who has such dreams is that the dream is actually referring to said events or people. What I learned from the analysis of my recurring dreams is that recent events and familiar happenings and persons are used to invoke interest and to find easy material for putting together dream plots. Dreams rarely present their elements with the meaning familiar to the dreamer. It should be added here that the rebus method has been used as a vehicle of dream communication with this author, and it applied mainly to illumination dreams (to be discussed presently.) Since dream transmissions are a kind of person-to-person communication the use of other forms of symbolization cannot be ruled out for dreamers with different backgrounds.

If the significance of the messages of dreams is so portentous, why should we have so much difficulty in grasping them? Why in a straight-forward manner do they not tell us what they mean? There are good reasons for the recourse to taciturnity. What needs to be said in this connection at this point is that dream messages are subject to the laws of continuity. Depending on the intellectual development of dreamers, a certain amount of time must lapse before a person can assimilate a different state of reality. A sudden demand for change can cause confusion, if not disorientation. A teenager knows himself by the physical features he has seen of himself in the mirror daily. If one day the mirror presented him instead with the shape that would appear sixty years later, obviously he would become unhinged.

Psychological changes are no easier. The psyche needs familiarity and continuity. Introducing it to a different kind of order of reality just does not set well. This is perhaps the reason that in Zen Buddhism, Koan is used to encourage monks to abandon their ultimate dependence on words and reason to force them to gain enlightenment. From this perspective, symbols are akin to Koan. The difference between dreams symbols and Koan may be that in the latter enlightenment reportedly appears suddenly.

Such is not the case with regard to dream symbolism which induces a gradual awareness and insight.

The Dream's Method of Guidance

Dreams aim at teaching reality with the intent of clarifying the true nature of human identity and that of the Divine. To this end, they generally use four methods: dissuasion, persuasion, illumination, and elaboration.

Based on the feedback from our dreams, the identity we think we have is false or a pseudo identity. This causes a great deal of anxiety, frustration, and pain. In this instance, dreams do not use a rebus. They use a dramatic piece or play as a striking metaphor. The painful emotions of the day are staged for us to know how, due to our wrong sense of reality; we suffer and need to give up these false expectations and beliefs that have ingrained themselves in us. Terrifying, shocking, shameful, brutal or unsightly scenes are presented to make us aware of what our pseudo-identity does to us and to dissuade us from such trammels. For instance, our feeling of helplessness may be shown by a wall closing in on us or by an attack of a monster or ferocious animals. The hurt feeling we experience in social situations may be depicted by our child being run over by a car. There is no relationship between our helplessness in waking and being attacked by an animal or between the hurt feeling and the car accident other than the emotions involved are similar. Our dreams tell us that we, because of misconceptions, resulting from mistaken identity, suffer unwarrantedly. Dissuasion dreams may discourage us from our customary precarious patterns of living by presenting us with such dreams as driving recklessly with defective eyesight and not knowing where we are going, or treading a surface under which is empty space.

The dreams that most dramatically bring to our notice our pseudo-identity are nightmares. These dreams are associated with such intense anxiety that dreamers suffering from them would often rather stay up all night than to go to sleep and experience a reoccurrence of them. Shakespeare expressed these nightmares thus:

> *"O' I passed a miserable night*
> *So full of ugly sights, of ghastly dreams,*
> *That, as I am a Christian faithful man,*
> *I would not spend another such night.*
> *Though it would to bring a world of happy days."*
> *Richard III, act I, scene IV*

Our dreams make us aware not only of our deficits and state of separation but also of our progress toward integration. By dissuasion dreams, we are challenged to review our fruitless ways of life and make necessary adjustments. By persuasion dreams, we are encouraged and given feedback that we are moving on the right track or that our efforts toward self-integration are authentic. The following verbal dream illustrates this type of persuasion or encouraging dreams.

- *Considerable progress has been made.*
- *You can do that, you can be cooperative.*
- *You describe it very well.*

Illumination dreams serve to inspire or enlighten us by providing us with a kind of knowledge that is relevant to our major life goals and of which we were hitherto in the dark. This category of dreams is often in more plain language. The examples cited in the rest of this book are typical of illumination dreams. Here we quote a few such dreams:

- *You are there in order to be born.*
- *The symbol is the best thing in the world that man has created.*
- *You have a problem because you still do not know who your companion is.*
- *What do you really have that may be taken away from you?*
- *You will be at home with yourself and the world when you come to recognize your company.*

New knowledge that dreams impart is often not immediately grasped by the dreamer. Gaining a new perspective of reality is a slow and arduous process. Elaboration dreams keep repeating points or principles that had been contained in previous dreams so that they are either better comprehended or they are further punctuated. As a rule, the concepts conveyed by dreams are unorthodox or unheard of. If they were common knowledge, dreams would become redundant. It may take hundreds of repetitions to put across such concepts as:

- *The other is indeed the other side of yourself.*
- *You forget that two makes one.*

Readers who have a sincere interest in learning from their dreams, naked truths about themselves, and the ultimate reality should prepare themselves for a long arduous journey. For one thing, dreams are personal; hence no two persons will have the same pattern in their dreams. Thus there is no cookbook approach to aid us in understanding them. By presenting us with inscrutable puzzles, dreams frustrate us mercilessly so that gradually our blindness may turn into the gift of clear seeing. If we are persistent and patient eventually our dreams will shed some light on our path, but only that degree of enough light to sustain our interests. Finding truth about our genuine identity and ultimate reality call for an unending quest. It never reaches the stage of completion or finality. Thus, as Frederich S. Perls points out: "To suffer one's death (of the old self-concept) and to be reborn (into a new being) is not easy." *Inside parentheses added.*

It is not very difficult to figure out the meaning of dissuasion dreams or dreams associated with violent emotions. As noted earlier such dreams are largely metaphorical. They tell us that our make-believe identity is the source of the emotional pain that we are suffering. To get rid of these pains, one has to let go of false belief systems. Illumination dreams should be examined from the angles of the rebus, charades, pun, or, in some contexts, in their literal sense. In fact, it would be helpful initially to consider all persons and objects in dreams as representing some aspects of our own personality.

It will also be useful to follow these guidelines: 1) suggest to yourself before falling asleep that you are really eager to have more dreams and want to remember them, 2) have a pad and a pen beside the bed to record your dreams as soon as they occur, 3) collect a larger number of dreams, and as far as possible, classify, analyze, and review them for consistency in their themes and symbols, 4) refrain from editing your dreams, if you find them disjointed or incoherent, and, 5) guess the meaning of symbols that are puzzling you and see whether dreams of subsequent nights will corroborate your guess. But we must hold our conclusion tentatively.

In the end, one sure thing is that we will be amply paid for our efforts if we work on our dreams long enough and persistently enough.

Summary

It is of prime importance to know reality. If we do not know what is real and what is illusion, we lead the ship of life without a helm. Dreams give us a glimpse of reality. Through dreams we gain a first-hand account of what is real and what is not. Freud and his followers hold that instigators such as thirst, hunger, sexual urge, urinary need, auditory experience, or daytime concerns beget dreams. Based on my experience, dreams are revelations. Their sources are an extra empirical or superior intellectual entity that for the lack of a better word is called "God." Thus dreams are messages from God. Through them, He communes with us directly. However, it is extremely difficult to understand dreams. They are mostly nebulous, mind-shattering and sense-transcending events. For the purpose of promoting an understanding of reality; apparently such enigmatic language is necessary.

To understand dreams, in addition to perseverance and dedication, we must have recourse to three aids 1) the themes about which dreams communicate to us, 2) knowledge of symbolic language and 3) knowledge of dreams' methods of guidance. First, we should know that dreams talk about three areas: self or human identity, the Divine or Supreme Being identity, and life purposes or human tasks. Any person, object, place or event that is used by dreams speaks only of these three areas, although initially the dreamer's own predicament is mainly addressed. Second, almost every image in the dream is a symbol. It stands for something other than what we know it to be. And symbols are generally personal. The view that there are universal symbols that mean the same thing to all mankind everywhere seems unwarrantable and assumptive. Symbols are included in the dream mainly as vehicles to communicate latent meaning by baffling our ordinary use of reasoning. For this author, symbols were mostly in rebus form. Finding the real referent for symbols requires great patience and perseverance. Third, overall, dreams are of four types: dissuasion dreams that discourage us from spending time on fruitless, self-defeating pursuits; persuasive dreams that encourage our efforts when we are on the right path; illumination dreams that furnish us with indispensable guidelines or information about fundamentals of life; and elaboration dreams which, like an understanding teacher, keep repeating and explaining points we have had difficulty following previously.

Dreams have to be understood through the test of self-consistency. Messages must be consistent both within each dream and with other dreams of the individual. Once we thoroughly understand the messages of the dreams, the scales of early misconception will fall from our eyes, and new vistas to reality will become open to us. Thus dreams have profound implications upon the way we lead out lives.

Chapter 2

The Nature of the Self

History reveals men's deeds and their outward character but not themselves.
There is a secret self that has its own life, unpenetrated and unguessed.

~Edward Bulwer-Lytton

We behold that which we are. We are that which we behold.

~Ruysbroeck

BASED ON THE conclusion drawn from a wealth of our received dreams, the key to understanding reality is understanding ourselves. Reality is the capstone of the realization of self-knowledge. The odd thing about the concepts of the self is that although everyone is sure of possessing it, although it is nearer to us than the jugular vein, and although we refer to it more than any other term, very few really know what it is. Hence, it has been impossible to deal realistically with the problems facing our lives. No parent, teacher, philosopher, psychology professor has ever told us exactly of what the self consists. Philosophers and psychologists have inadvertently added to the confusion by proposing various and, at times, contradictory definitions for the term "self." In the absence of a precise definition those who seek to know themselves are obviously left with no recourse. In the last analysis, we are not in any proper sense a genuine human being until we first find out what it means to have a true human identity. So long as we have not attained such an identity, we struggle in life blindly; worse, we remain unaware of our blindness. Consequently, no meaningful social reform or no real advancement and growth are in the cards for us.

Throughout the long history of civilization, human beings have been curious about the causes of their conduct or the agent that regulates, guides, and controls their behavior and thought. In particular, philosophers, more than the ordinary people, have been preoccupied with the phenomenon, termed "self." Even the best minds have had difficulty defining the self-objectively because they could not find other related concepts that could explain its nature in more familiar terms. The most common term used for expressing this center of personal identity was the "soul." In the context of religious thought, the soul was considered to be free, of divine origin, and also immortal. The common concept was that the soul shaped human destiny. Some philosophers regarded self and mind to be synonymous. They equated self as a subject with the mind and the self as an object with the body or held the self as a body-mind unity. Other synonyms that have been used for the term of self include: spirit, ego, agent, subject, psyche, knower, person, and, of course, the first person "I."

The oldest text that deals with the concept of the self is the Upanishads that are believed to have been composed beginning in 500 B.C. based on teachings circulated since 1000 B.C. The text mainly embodies the wisdom of the ancient mystics and constitutes the highest authority for Hindu beliefs. According to the Upanishads, "self is all, self is one, self is everywhere, self is all beings, and all beings are the self." It is specific that "self is within all and without all….Self moves swifter than thought. It is fleeting, traveling, formless; it takes the form of objects in which it dwells and makes many forms of itself." Regarding the relation of the self with Brahman, the Upanishads reveal that "self and Brahman are one, self is within and Brahman is without." Strange as some of these pronouncements may seem, some of them reappear in different forms in the received dreams to be quoted.

Self from the Perspective of Philosophers

The philosopher who was best known for his thirst for self-knowledge was Socrates (470-399 B.C.) He felt he was called to shore up the ethical dimension of life by the admonition "know thyself." He believed that self as a whole is something more than the parts; something that appears to be transcendental or in some sense divine. Another well-known philosopher who showed great interest in the nature of the self was Rene Descartes (1596-

1650). He began methodically doubting knowledge based on authority, sense and reason, in the hope of arriving at the end at something indutable. Thus he arrived at his famous *"Cogito ergo sum"* (I think, therefore I am), or so long as I think, so long certainly I exist , although I might immediately cease to exist if once I were to stop thinking. "I am then, to speak with precision, a thing which thinks that is to say a mind, an understanding or a reason."[1]

The English philosopher, John Locke (1632-1704), a founder of pragmatism, defined self as "a conscious thinking thing" similar to that of Descartes' definition. However, Locke made a distinction between the self and the person. He held that when one is seen from the outside by others, the term "person" is appropriate. He stated, "I am self only myself and am person for others." George Berkeley (1685-1753), an Irish Bishop, who was influenced substantially by Locke, considered self, soul, spirit, all as synonymous. He largely used the term spirit and defined it as a perceiving, acting being.

David Hume (1711-1776), a well-known Scottish philosopher, was unable to discover any permanent self. Introspection discloses only fleeting perceptions. He said, "When I enter most intimately into what I call myself, I never can catch myself at any time without a perception and never observe anything but perception." He concluded that the self is a mere bundle of perceptions or the perceptions must be the same with self, since one cannot survive the other. He was also convinced that the self and synthetic power were names for nothing but actual connection between ideas. About the same time, Immanuel Kant (1724-1804), the foremost thinker of the Enlightenment, held that the higher powers are the sole organizers of conscious life, and the name he gave to the totality of the individual self was "character."[2] He did not elaborate on the nature of the self either.

Three more modern philosophers, who have briefly referred to the nature of the self, are Hegel, Bergson, and Buber. GWF Hegel (1770-1831), who marked the pinnacle of Post-Kantian German idealism, set forth a dynamic conception of a self that is so interrelated with the environment that a clear-cut distinction cannot be made between the two. He held that the self is experiencing reality at all times, but all finite persons are absorbed into an absolute which transcends personality. French philosopher, Henri

Bergson (1859-1941), a founder of Process philosophy, believed that "self is something which changes but doesn't cease...for a self that does not change does not endure...there is one reality, which we all seize from within...it is our own personality in its flowing through time. It is our self which endures."[3] Finally Martin Buber (1878-1965), a German Jewish philosopher, in his book, *I and Thou,* detailed that through the *thou,* a man becomes an *I.* He emphasized that the world and I are mutually inclusive.[4]

Self from the Perspective of Psychologists

In the 19th century in Germany, psychologists were very preoccupied with the study of self or soul, endeavoring to find a scientific base for it. Since the middle of the 19th century, psychologists have had to decide whether to identify with scientists and deal with observable and verifiable data or with philosophers. Apparently preferring the respectability attached to science and winking at the fact that their appellation came from psych-logia (soul knowledge), they opted to become scientists. Subsequently, psychologists eschewed discussions of such topics as self, ego, consciousness, and mind because such concepts are not amenable to systematic, accurate observation and as such were ruled to be false issues. Thus, with the rise of scientific psychology, the study of the self, per se, has been firmly rejected.

Inevitably, a number of psychologists have felt the need for dealing with the term self and therefore attempted to set forth a definition for it. As a result, two distinct concepts have appeared or reappeared: (1) The self is regarded as a group of psychological processes which govern behavior, and (2) the self is defined as the individual's attitude and feeling toward himself or the individual as known to himself. Also some have made a distinction between self and ego. The prevalent view is that the self is what one is aware about himself while the ego is applied to the total mental processes, namely, perceiving, thinking, remembering, etc. There is no general agreement as to the precise way in which these two terms should be used.

Some psychologists and sociologists have put forward a somewhat more subtle definitions of self. Mention needs to be made here of the ones which are better known. Wilhelm Wundt's view was that the mental processes in their totality are what should be designated by the term self. According to William James, the self is a composite of thoughts and feelings, which constitute a person's awareness of his individual existence, his conception of who and what he is. A person's self is the "sum total of all that he can call his body, traits and abilities, his material possessions, his family, his friends, his enemies, his vocation, vocabulary, and much more."[5] Gardner Murphy employed the term ego, which he defined as a system of habitual activities that enhance or defend the self. He also defined the self as "the individual as known to the individual."

Harry Stack Sullivan, who emphasized the impact of the social relationship on the development of the self, considered self as "that to which we refer when we say 'I.' It is the custodian of awareness; it is the thing about a person, which has awareness and alertness, which notices what goes on, and which notices what goes on in its field."[6] For George Herbert Mead, self was an object of awareness rather than a system of processes. A person does not regard himself as an object. He learns to think of himself as others respond to him. The self is essentially a social structure, and it arises in social experience. It is impossible to conceive of a self arising outside of social experience.

Karen Horny, who is mostly concerned with the healthy person or authentic self, remarks that the concept of the self provides a key to the understanding of mental health. The healthy individual is true to himself and has integrity within himself. If there is a valid and real attitude toward the self, that attitude will manifest as valid and real toward others.[7]

In his book, *Self and Others,* R.D. Lang sees a discrepancy between a self as being for oneself and a self as being for others. He postulates that one's self-identity is the story one tells one's self of who one is. We learn to be who we are told we are. Self is not what others take one to be. Attribution by others prevents the development of a realistic sense of self. Carl Roger, the founder of the client-centered therapy, held that the self consists of a pattern of conscious perceptions and values of the "I" and "me." He found unacceptable a view of men driven by social impulses that he suppresses only with great effort. Roger believed that in every individual, there is a drive toward self-actualization.[8]

Freud was not concerned with the concept of the self. His construction of personality was made up of three major systems: the id, the ego, and the superego. The id was regarded as the original system of personality.

It was considered to be the true unconscious or the deepest part of the psyche. The ego was that aspect of the psyche that was conscious and most in touch with the external reality. The superego was described as a system within the total psyche developed by incorporating the parental standards as perceived by the ego.

Carl Gustav Jung, the founder of the field of analytical psychology, defined the self as the totality of conscious and unconscious psyche. He maintained that this totality transcended our vision. It is not definable; its existence is merely postulated and nothing can be predicted as to its possible content. It would be widely arbitrary and unscientific to restrict the self to the limits of the individual psyche. Jung considered the center of personality to be the self and also referred to the self as the summation of the personality. As shall be seen, some of Jung's views of the self coincide with those of the received dreams.

Self from the Perspective of the Dreams

One of the three themes of the received dreams is the reality or nature of the self. Dreams point out that we do not know who we are but believe that we know ourselves. We know we have a body with certain features. We have seen these features in the mirror and have identified with them since we were very young. Furthermore, most of us think this image we see in the mirror shows our identity, expressing clearly who we are. We think that skin is our boundary and all that we are is contained within this bag of skin. Of course, we know we have grown and have changed physically, but the changes that have occurred have been at such a slow pace that we do not notice any difference in our outward features from day to day, even from year to year. The received dreams disclose that what we see in the mirror and what we think is inside us is not all of us. We are much more than that; even more than the best of what we can think. Therefore, the first thing that our received dreams emphasize is that we have no real self as it is evident from the following dream statements:

- *What you think is yourself is not yourself.*
- *You need to know your real self.*
- *To know the self is to know reality.*
- *The ID you carry is not valid, you must obtain a new ID.*

- *You are more or less like a magnetic tape on which words and events of your past life have been recorded. Those records motivate you throughout life.*
- *You are held captive by what you have learned.*
- *Your belief system is your owner now.*
- *So long as you do not know yourself, you cannot be of much use to yourself or others.*
- *You are wearing artificial legs. With those, you cannot go very far.*
- *Dreams aim at presenting you with your real self.*

Initially the received dreams have not been as concise and explicit as those quoted here, nor have they been in verbal form. To make us aware that we have no genuine self, our first dreams are narratives or events of a bizarre or frightening nature. As mentioned in the previous chapter, our bizarre thoughts are depicted for us in a bizarre fashion.

It is not hard to agree with the position of the received dreams regarding a lack of genuine human identity. All of us were once children lacking discrimination, and like a tape recorder, recorded what we heard, and like a camera took picture of what we saw. The recording and pictures thus acquired largely laid the foundation of our personality, our reality, our self, or worldview. In order to survive and maintain our sanity, we had to adhere to the reality thus destined. We develop one sense of reality or another depending on who our parents are and in what cultures we are reared. The reality of a child born to certain religious group may dictate that he should go to war, or commit suicide by detonating a bomb so that he may enter paradise forthwith. The reality of a child in the Western culture may prescribe that the goal of life is to become successful or rich.

A good many individuals in all cultures modify their early conditioning, but no one can change their identity to something inconceivable. As we shall see, the dreams that the author has had direct attention to the fact that the self or our real identity is that thing which is beyond us. Such a teaching seldom has appeared anywhere; hence, a self that embodies such a worldview is inevitably rare. Consequently, the received dreams, in a great variety of forms, remind us that the self we think we have is the reflection parental and cultural influences. In other words, it is fictitious or something that exists only in our imaginations.

Self as Consciousness

The dreams received by this author are more specific about the nature of the self than the views expressed by the writers included in the previous section. Dreams under study simply equate the conception of the self with that of consciousness. However, the term consciousness itself is an unfortunate one on account of its ambiguity, in spite of the fact that Descartes stated, "I can doubt anything but my consciousness." Although this phenomenon is in many ways the most familiar thing that each of us possesses, it also remains one of the least understood concepts. One thing is sure: no conscious process has been experienced by any part of the body, nor has any investigator found its seat in the brain. Titchener was convinced that he could unravel the secret of consciousness by understanding the operation of the nervous system. However, his research in this area was without the desired result. Titchener's definition of consciousness was the sum total of mental processes occurring now.[9]

Due to its ambiguity, use of the term consciousness has been abandoned by behaviorists, substituting attention for it. J.B. Watson gave up the term consciousness of behavior as a starting point for his theory. An early behaviorist facetiously remarked that consciousness is like yonder clouds "almost in the shape of a camel…backed like a weasel…very much like a whale; in short, something of which no scientific truth can be asserted with the means at our control."[10] In some respect, the rejection of consciousness by psychologists may have arisen from such definition as that of Heraclitus, who called consciousness, "an enormous space, whose boundaries, even by traveling along every path, could never be found out."[11]

On the other hand, Buddhists and Indian mystics consider the whole reality as consciousness. It is said that there is no seed of Buddhism when there is no consciousness. Like existentialists, Eastern mystics believe consciousness is co-extensive with the totality of being. The Indian philosopher Sankara considers consciousness as one without a second.[12]

Also monistic idealists hold that the world or reality exists essentially as consciousness rather than sensory things, and all objects we see are already in consciousness, which is believed to be primary. Their one-liner reads: "Consciousness is the ground of all being and our self-consciousness is *that* consciousness."[13] In the 17th century, Thomas Hobbes reduced consciousness to motion, and anticipating Titchener, Hobbes identified it with the changes in the nervous system. He asserted that consciousness is only the feeling of changes in the brain.[14] The definition given by Locke for consciousness was "the perception of what passes in a man's own mind." He specified that consciousness or reflection is a person's observing or noticing the internal operations of his mind.

Descartes stressed that the essence of mind or consciousness is thought. But Leibniz vastly enlarged this viewpoint. Hitherto consciousness had been taken to mean that of which one is distinctly conscious. Leibniz stated that below the threshold of clear consciousness there is a dark background of obscure consciousness, petite perception, or unconscious mental states.[15] We might say Leibniz anticipated Freud in introducing the phenomenon of the "unconscious state." Leibniz also maintained that consciousness is a form of memory. Hegel's standpoint was that consciousness is a synthetic organization or integration of bodily function.

According to Bergson, the task of consciousness is to create something at every moment. Agreeing with Husserl's principle that consciousness is always conscious of something, Sartre emphasized that there is consciousness only if something appears to it. If nothing appears, as presumably in death, then there is no longer any consciousness.[16] Heidegger's viewpoint is that conscience (consciousness) is the awareness of how it is with oneself. For William James, consciousness does not exist as a substance distinct from its contents. It is a grouping. The organism selects from the objects in its environment those to which it gives attention; the objects thus selected form a group. Consciousness is simply the name for this grouping of objects.

Some physicists regard consciousness as necessary for bringing forth reality. Eugen Wigner is well-known for saying, "It is not possible to formulate the laws of quantum mechanics without reference to consciousness."[17] He also notes, "The reality of my perception, sensation, consciousness is immediate and absolute." In a way quantum physicists speak of consciousness and self as part of the quantum process. They claim that "consciousness is the agency that collapses the wave of the quantum objects"…and some remarked "nothing is outside consciousness." Physicist Amit Goswami, like monistic idealists, speaks of consciousness as the ground of all being and considers in a sense everything to be consciousness.

In many respects, the received dreams embody some of the points expressed by above thinkers, but this author finds the position of the received dreams different and novel. The dreams do not appear to make a distinction between the term "self" and the term "consciousness." In effect, they are used interchangeably. Thus, in order to make known the nature of the self the received dreams direct attention to the concept of consciousness as it is evident from the following dream statements:

- *Since self is consciousness, you must start with consciousness.*
- *Description of the self is consciousness.*
- *You find yourself as you learn more about the nature of consciousness.*
- *Your dreams make known that you and your whole being are of the nature of consciousness.*
- *You can say being is consciousness*
- *Consciousness is of what you are conscious.*
- *You are merely a conscious being.*

These dreams will be further elaborated upon as we consider other dreams to be included in this chapter and the next. What we can conclude from the dreams quoted above is that human identity or self from one aspect is tantamount to consciousness.

Consciousness as Seeing

If the self is equivalent to our consciousness, we need to form a conception of the term "consciousness." Based on the specific contents of our dreams, consciousness is equivalent to the act of "seeing." This definition indicates that the verb "seeing" must be taken with its widest range of meaning. According to the Random House Dictionary, the verb "to see" has some thirty different meanings, including to have experience, to be aware of, to recognize, to perceive the meaning, to attend, to learn or find by observation, to direct one's attention, to apprehend object by sight, to perceive, to take note, to think, to arrive at a conclusion, and much more. Thus the term "seeing" as used here should be considered with all other meanings of the same term. Specifically, four senses of the gerund "seeing" are significant in relation to our dreams, namely to be aware of, to sense, to think, and to direct one's attention.

For Philo, sight or seeing is an exact image of the soul, since, according to him, eyes show every change of thought and feeling. According to D.T. Suzuki, seeing is regarded as the basis of knowing in all Buddhist schools and also as a source of enlightenment. According to our dreams, conscious life is coextensive with seeing when seeing is regarded with its widest range of meaning.

A variety of terms has been used by other authors to designate consciousness, including mind, identity, sensation, cognition, memories, self-experience, brain processes, soul, thinking, sensing, knowing, perceiving, feeling, and discriminating. Based on the impression we have from the received dreams all these terms fall under the general category of the act of "seeing."

The received dreams do not specify that consciousness and seeing are synonymous but use both terms to refer to the concept of the self. When there are two things, each equal to a third, logically they must be interchangeable. Here are some dreams which equate the term self with the gerund seeing:

- *Self is seeing.*
- *Use seeing when you mean self.*
- *To be is to see.*
- *Your being ends when seeing ends.*
- *The self comes about as we see things.*
- *The self as seeing is not a thing.*
- *You need to recognize yourself to be a process, not a state.*

To make known the nature of the self, the received dreams seem to give preferences to the term "seeing" than the term "consciousness," apparently for the reason that the first term is based on a verb and the latter is a noun. The structure of self whether defined as consciousness or seeing, is dynamic; hence, a verb form explains it best. Mention needs to be made here that Berkeley also pointed out that mind (consciousness) is a perceiving, active being. It is also noteworthy to add that some philosophers opined that consciousness cannot be truly described in terms of anything else. Such it is not the position of our dreams which define consciousness as that which sees. A few dreams that speak to the fluid nature of seeing are:

- *Succession of seeing events makes up for the self.*
- *Self is a process of converting.*
- *Through motion, self as seeing comes into being.*
- *Self or seeing is a constant transformation.*
- *You travel continuously from one place to another; as a result, you as self come into being.*
- *Change is the reality of the self.*

We must remember that Heraclitus held that sensation depended upon motion and the world is nothing but a process of change and becoming. Nothing remains untouched or immune to change. The persistence of unity despite constant change is depicted by his famous analogy of the life of a river: "upon those who step into the same rivers different waters flow down." Also Aristotle's main topic of psychology was motion. He declared that the conscious being is always active. Even in physics, there has been a shift of emphasis from object to events.[18] Overall, the dynamic relationship has been accepted as part of the quantum theory. The topic of self and motion will be considered further in the next chapter.

Self as "I am that I am"

It was mentioned above that our received dreams first equated the self with consciousness and then consciousness with the gerund seeing with its wide range of meanings. In this section, we quote a number of verbal dreams that all indicate that the self as seeing is really its content. The dreams leave no ambiguity here. They say the self is what it sees or what it has seen, or we are what we see now or what we have seen in the past. The implication of this definition that "the self is that which it sees" is vast. For one thing, it means that in a special sense that which we see at any moment is "part of us." How can this be explained? If our essence is the activity of seeing and if seeing materializes only when it has a concrete object as its content, the concrete object must be regarded as the necessary element of the activity seeing. Thus, at any given moment, the self consists of the act of seeing plus the object it sees.

Some philosophers like Bertrand Russell say that the object itself is not part of seeing or perception. Our received dreams consider the concrete object itself as part of the self or seeing, since seeing divorced from its content will have no existence. In this way, the received dreams make the discovery of our identity easy. If we want to know who we are, we have to look and see what we have in front of our eyes now or had in front of our eyes in the past. If now we see a mountain, we are the act of seeing plus the mountain. If we are thinking about the school we attended, then at this moment we are the thought or the seeing of that school plus the school itself, as the thought of the school cannot materialize without the actual school. An analogy might make this point more clear. As the image in the mirror cannot exist without something in front of it; the act of seeing cannot come about without a piece of the outer world. The two go together all the time. Preposterous as this may seem; it is what our received dreams evidently put forth regarding the nature of the self. One might conclude if such is the case then the self is not confined in the body alone. The received dreams seem to suggest exactly that. This topic will be taken up again in chapter 4.

The following received dreams are good examples as to how the author of dreams keeps elaborating its central message by repeating it in various forms. The pronoun "that," as used in the received dreams, is a general term that refers to what is immediately present to us or anything that is the object of seeing.

- *Human beings are conscious due to objects they see beyond them.*
- *You are that which you see.*
- *What you see is your identity.*
- *Seeing is the seeing of that.*
- *You are the seeing of that which you see.*
- *See yourself as that which is seen.*
- *You have no other way to know yourself but through that.*
- *Say: What is there is me.*
- *Seeing emerges from the presence of that.*
- *That shows your identity in thousand different ways (as each object becomes yourself at the moment seen).*
- *That which you see is a mirror that reflects who you really are.*

- *What is unknown here becomes known there.*
- *Whatever you see is your picture.*
- *In a sense, you are the carrier of what you see or what you have seen.*
- *The seen reveals the identity of the seer.*
- *That needs to be there at all times so that one will be able to know oneself.*
- *Self is that which you see standing there.*
- *What is here stands there.*
- *The external objects are your referent.*
- *When the referent changes you change too.*
- *Self is there. The substance of your inner side is the outer side.*
- *Whatever you have seen in front of your is the measure of what is in the back of you.*
- *You become a being after seeing that. No outside, no inside.*
- *The objects you see beget your inner side successively.*

Ideas akin to what was outlined above in one form or another have been floating around since the time of the Greeks. Heraclitus remarked: "We perceive any particular thing because we are that thing." But none seems to be as patent as those quoted here. In the Upanishads, we find such passages as "that which is seen in the eye—that is the Self."[19] In philosophy, some idealists have expressed the view that an object and ideas are one, and dualism of matter and mind is incoherent and impossible. For example, Josiah Royce says, "The whole world of ideas is essentially one world and so it is essentially the world of the self and that art thou." When you aim at yonder object, you are really saying "I, as my real self, as my larger self, as my complete consciousness, already in the deepest truth possess that object."[20]

The foremost exponent of existentialism, Jean-Paul Sartre, wrote: "Consciousness is always conscious of something….All things that the individual human comes into contact with are phenomena for his consciousness." Alfred Schultz, Austrian-American sociologist and philosopher, pointed out that "existing objects constitute the causes of our cognition or consciousness." In the same vein, William Hocking explained that "mind is its content." The end result of it all is that the more we think about that which we call "the self," like Hume, the more we find the self nowhere, except in that which is seen or about which is thought.

Summary

In this chapter, an attempt was made to explain the nature of the self based on thousands of verbal dreams the author has had over a long period of time. Who we really are has always been uppermost in the mind of the average person, and in particular it has been in the minds of philosophers and psychologists. The latter group of thinkers have expressed their thoughts on the topic, using their own as well as the cultural wisdom of their time. The common characteristics of the viewpoints of these thinkers are that they are constructive speculations, but no agreed definition about the concept of the self has emerged that could lead to a greater understanding of the matter. One reason for this is that the nature of the self is perhaps the most baffling and mysterious phenomena with which the logical mind has ever had to deal. The material presented in this chapter about the nature of the self are based on explicit and consistent messages that the author has received over the past forty years. These dreams appear to render the concept of the self rather as clean-cut as it can be made. They simply say that the self of any individual is that which he or she sees at any instant or what he or she has seen in the past.

The way the received dreams elucidate the meaning of the self is intriguing. First, they equate the self with consciousness, then consciousness with the gerund seeing, using seeing with its widest range of meanings to include, thinking, perceiving, conceiving, knowing or all mental functioning. The conclusion drawn is that if the self is identical with the act of seeing, and seeing consists of its content; hence, the self is also its content. In other words, we, as conscious, seeing beings, always require the presence of another in order to possess a self. Numerous dreams were quoted to pinpoint the fact that without content or without a physical object, seeing or self cannot come about. Hence, the content or the object produces the inner, conscious side of the self. Obviously, this seems contrary to common sense. This means we are outside the body as well as inside it. Absurd as the conclusion appears to be, our received dreams are unequivocal about their dicta that the self is "what it sees" or borrowing a phrase from the Bible, "I am that I am." The next chapter will expand the definition given above of the self.

Chapter 3

The Structure of the Self

The relation between the organism and the object results in a conscious condition.

~Pierre Jean Cabanas

The Self stands over against the world.

~John Macmurray

IN THE PRECEDING chapter, our received dreams equated the self with consciousness, and consciousness with the gerund "seeing" when seeing is taken in its broadest sense to include such mental activities as thinking, knowing, sensing, focusing, being aware, and many more. The dreams quoted clearly reveal that our identity or our self comes into being at each instant based on the things we see at that instant. In essence, this means that the self as seeing is its object. The thing that is there brings about what is here. Obviously, common sense tells us that seeing is an internal event and the object we see is an external thing. One is here, and the other is out there. How could something far away constitute our self, our consciousness, or our seeing? If they are of two different kinds of phenomenon, how then could they interact? This chapter aims at answering these questions again based on the specific messages of a host of received dreams.

Self as a Bimodal Entity

A number of the received dreams express the fact that the self has two halves, an inner half that functions as the seeing side of the self and an outer half that functions as the objective or seen side of the self. The two halves are complementary, yet each has a different function and constitution. The terms generally used for each side include: manifest and unmanifest, evident and hidden, visible and invisible, physical and non-physical, outer and inner, there and here, non-living and living, unseeing and seeing, ground and unground, real and ideal, self in particular and self in general, phenomenal world and super-phenomenal world, and many more. For most of us, it is obvious that we have a side that we do not see, and although it is hidden it exerts a great influence on us. But if we are asked to point out the locus of this hidden part, few of us, if any, know the answer. The received dreams have provided an answer to this question, which will be considered later in this chapter. Below we cite a number of dreams that speak unambiguously of the two sides of the self.

- *Seeing requires two sides.*
- *Your reality consists of a side which is conscious and a side which is unconscious.*
- *You are like an entity half of which is alive and half of which is dead.*
- *The living side of you has a counterpart which by itself is dead.*
- *The outer half of you should bear the label "the dead half."*
- *One half of the self is visible and another half is invisible.*
- *There you find the outer half of yourself.*

Thus, the self is a mixed form of being. It is physical and non-physical; it is one and many. The two sides are different aspects of the same thing, as the wave and the particle are different aspects of quantum phenomena.

The significance of the dreams cited above is their emphasis on the fact that we as self have a side which is visible and a side which is invisible; the latter side is seeing and living, whereas the former side is unseeing and non-living. Humans as visible entities are living and seeing due to their connection with the invisible side. What was set out by our received dreams seems to agree with the worldview of Plato who said, "The mind alone sees and hears; all else is deaf and blind."[1] Apparently, what our dreams intend by the inner half is what Plato referred to as the mind. On the other hand, the position of our received dreams is similar to a modern trend in physics. Lawrence H. Domash writes: "Where previously the world of physics consisted of sensory, measurable experience, quantum mechanics introduced the wave function level that is by nature real but unmanifest…a world quite different from every day experience."[2] Fritjof Capra remarked: "In the deeper realm of an atom one discovers a different reality behind the superficial, mechanistic appearance."[3]

Other physicists who have referred to this unmanifest world as consciousness and have considered consciousness to be necessary for understanding the physical world include Niels Bohr, Werner Heisenberg, Erwin Schrodinger, David Bohm, Doug Seeley, Michael Baker, and Eugen Wigner. In this connection, Wigner observes:

> "There are several reasons for return, on the part of most physical scientists, to the spirit of Descartes' *'Cognito ergo sum,'* which reorganizes thought, that is, mind as primary….When the province of physical theory was extended to encompass microscopic phenomena, through the creation of quantum mechanics, the concept of the consciousness came to the fore again: it was not possible to formulate the laws of quantum mechanics in a fully consistent way without reference to the consciousness."[4]

It is no surprise that physicists have discovered that mind or consciousness is essential for understanding the nature of things, and a different reality exists behind the superficial or visible phenomena. The computer does not invent itself. A drone does not empower itself to fly. It is the mind of scientists and technologists who conceive them and put them together, and mind is not a physical thing. Something physical is unable to think as Plato declared. Still the question remains: Where is the mind or the self?

Self as Motion

In the preceding section, it was noted that the self as a seeing entity has an inner side and an outer side. It was also mentioned that one of the issues that Descartes and other philosophers attempted to resolve was the relationship between mind and body. Many solutions have been proposed but none of them has stood the test of full consistency. Although the mind -body relationship is substantially different from the relationship between the inner and the outer side of the self as predicted by the received dreams, yet there is no doubt that both domains involve similar difficulties. How can the immaterial mind or the inner side of the self have any relationship with the material body or the outer, physical half of the self?

About 300 B.C., Zeno found an answer to this problem by saying "Between the perceiver and the perceived, there is movement or motion." Our received dreams seem to say the same thing when they point out that between the inner side of the self and the outer side runs motion or an exchange of energy. What we call the self is a flowing, irreversible succession of exchange between the two sides of the self. This flow cannot be ascribed either to the inner or the outer alone but rather to the interaction between them. In other words what mediates between the side which is non-physical and that which is physical is motion. The self has no abiding place anywhere. A shift of attention keeps the self as seeing in a state of dynamic flux. Thus, the self as that which sees, feels, knows, and experiences is not a thing; it is a process, a flux or motion, or a verb.

The view that the self is a form of motion or force has been set forth by many philosophers. Heraclitus, who did not specifically refer to the topic of self, maintained that all things are flowing. He said, "Nothing ever is, everything is becoming."[5] Also throughout his psychology, Aristotle spoke of motion, saying "In all sensation an objective stimulus is the cause of change which proceeds through a medium into consciousness." Aristotle's medium has been interpreted as being an atmosphere through which material species were transmitted. Likewise, Thomas Aquinas stressed that beings of our world are in movement. In the 16th century, Telesius, an Italian philosopher and natural scientist, held that the soul is of the nature of motion and that things or material conditions set in motion the soul. Bishop Berkeley also believed that the soul or spirit (self) was an active being.

Similarly, Schelling found in force common ground of nature and ego. He pointed out that the objective gave to consciousness what consciousness reproduced anew. Bergson, however, was first to elaborate on a process philosophy, embracing dynamic values such as motion, change, and evolution. He says:

"In reality, there is no separate solid things, only an endless stream of becoming…But becoming may be a movement up or a movement down; when it is a movement up is it called life; when it is a movement down it is…called matter….The movement up brings things together, while a movement down separates them."[6]

What our received dreams explicate about the nature of the self seems in some respects to be in accord with Bergson's position quoted above. Our received dreams specifically affirm that the self is a motion between its inner half and the outer half. In the dreams quoted below, the pronoun "you" is often used instead of the term "self."

- *Self is an operation or activity.*
- *Self materializes as it makes the outer, the inner and the inner, the outer.*
- *You as seeing make two kinds of movement; ascending and descending.*
- *You go in a circuit successively.*
- *When you go there, there comes to you.*
- *You are like a bird that is lifeless when on the ground and alive when up in the air.*
- *You are like a creature that first is lifeless then becomes alive through movement.*
- *With magnetic force, you go up and you return with the same force.*
- *Like the motion of air in breathing, you are taken in and then out.*
- *As a bird, you move up and down and as you do so you determine both sides of you.*
- *Your self is like an elevator that is constantly moving upward and downward.*
- *In a covered space, you move through the air like a bird and as you do so you carry in your memory what you are seeing at that instant.*
- *You are something like energy. You come into being as you go up and come down moment by moment.*
- *As a seeing entity, you go up with the act of seeing and come down with the same act.*
- *That which successively goes up and returns constitutes you.*

- *The inner half comes into being through the action of the outer half and the latter becomes known through the action of the former.*
- *You have a self due to the interaction between your outer and inner halves.*
- *The outer half and the inner half create each other.*
- *The whole dynamic of the self consists of pulsation (vibration).*
- *The outer half emits some kind of vibration continually.*
- *Consider the outer half as energy*

The question often asked is why reality should express itself in two different modes or ways, while they have no effect on each other. How can two things with entirely different properties be said to be one and the same? The answer to this kind of question, based on the received reams, is that the self as seeing or as motion is a kind of tertium quid that encompasses both kinds of modes or both the seer and the seen. In other words, the self as consciousness or seeing is all-inclusive. It incorporates both its inner and outer halves.

The Model of the Self

In the previous chapter, we said that our received dreams identify the self with consciousness, consciousness with the act of seeing, and the act of seeing with that which is seen at any given moment. In the preceding section, it was explained that the self has two sides, a visible side and an invisible, and as these two sides interact with each other, the self as seeing comes into being. It was emphasized that the self is of the nature of a verb, not a noun, or of constant motion and change. It travels continually between its two sides. To help us visualize this rather complicated structure of the self, we need an analogy or a model that can call attention to the detailed arrangement it entails. To this end, Figure 1is presented below. No doubt the whole structure is considerably more involved, but, fortunately, we have had some guidance from our received dreams, both in regard to the form and to the notation of the model. Some dreams have shown that the structure of the self looks like lungs engaged in breathing. In other dreams, the shape is shown like a bowl turned upside-down or like an arched bridge, a dome of a mosque, a cone, or simply a hemisphere.

However, the configuration that is presented here as Figure 1 is the one that surfaced most in the dreams:

The Self as Motion

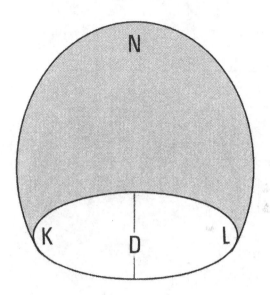

Figure 1: The inner and the outer interact in some regular, lawful way, to bring forth the self moment by moment.

According to Figure 1, the self as seeing represents interaction and motion. Through the act of seeing or moving, the self gives rise to its inner half (the invisible side (N)) as well as to its outer half (the visible side (D)). As a process first, the organism and the environment (K and L, conjoined together) ascend, and as a result bring forth the inner half. Then at any instant, the inner half, by focusing on different objects in sight, descends to make the outer half visible. As a kind of superposition, the inner half always makes for unity by incorporating its two constituents (K and L). The striking feature of the model is that it shows the self not to be in the body (K) alone; it shows the body is one of its fundamental constituents. The self as seeing acquires its inner half in a space outside and above the body and the object or above the organism and the environment.

To further illustrate the nature of the two halves of the self, one might say that they would express their existence thus: the inner half will say, "I am that because the outer half that consists of the coupling of organism and environment has given birth to me and made me into a seeing entity." The outer half might similarly say: "We were unknown, as such non-existent; we became something due to the vision of the inner half."

From the standpoint of motion, the model of the self is somewhat similar to that of the Chinese symbolism of Yin and Yang.

Tao in continous cyclic movement

The two sides, bright and dark, as the two aspects of the same reality, compliment and counterbalance each other through motion. However, in the end, both sides are represented in an all-embracing circle, the symbol of the final unity of Tao, or the correct divine way.

A word must be said about the notations used in Figure 1. Symbols N, D, K, and L are all dictated by our received dreams. I am sure that N stands for *un* or one, and D stands for *deux* or two. However, I am not so sure about the significance of the symbols K and L. Conceivably K is akin to the Egyptian *Ka*, the personality that was believed to be born with the individual. The individual spirit and vital force was also known as Ka in ancient Egypt. The symbol L may have reference to the Latin *ille* or French *il* or *elle*, signifying he, it, they and their. It is also probable that these symbols have all been arbitruarily designated as an aid for creation of rebuses or to provide suitable vehicles of communication. Insofar as these notations refer to Figure 1 and to the dreams to be quoted, we confirm that K stands for the individual or organism; L stands for the environment, others or whatever can become the object to the act of seeing at any moment; and D stands for the instances where K and L are taken together as a single thing with two phases or where the object and the image of the object are treated as the same.

The Locus and Function of the Components of the Self

As Figure 1 shows there is one self, which is two-fold or has two modes: an inner and an outer mode. The latter mode or half is also a pair of correlates. That is every visible or objective half comprises two elements: the organism (K) and the environment (L). Although they are two things, they are so related that one directly implies or is complimentary to the other.

The organism refers to the physiological make-up of the individual that is capable of receiving and storing images of the environment. The term "environment" mainly refers to the objects that have concrete form so that they can cast their images and can be seen or conceived. Our received dreams refer to the organism and the environment in combination as *that* or *object* or D or as just *two*. In actuality, the objective side of the self always subsists in a dyad or in a pair. They are so related that one directly implies the other.

Dreams specifying that the organism and the environment are two elements of the self include the following:

- *Regard the organism and the environment both as two objects.*
- *The concrete side of the self as seeing is a dyad.*
- *Call the organism and the environment as the objective side of the act of seeing.*
- *The organism and the environment hung as two loads from the inner half of the self.*
- *The outer side of the self as two mirrors show what is in the inner side of self.*
- *The two (the organism and the environment) make up one.*

- *The two objects of the self produce their inner side.*
- *The two objects are "double you" of the act of seeing.*
- *The two objects serve as a kind of vehicle for the inner half of the self.*

The Inner Side of the Self

The fact that we have an inner life is rather self-evident. Many terms have been used to refer to it—mind, knower, soul, spirit, ego, agent, etc. Several common words have been used by our received dreams to express the inner side of the self. These include soul, spirit, mind, psyche, and I; all of which indicate the presence of life, motion and activity. As the term "inner" implies, the inner side is that which lies behind appearance, consisting of the whole gamut of mental activities with which all of us are equipped. We know that which enjoys something delicious is not the tongue or stomach or brain. There is something else that we do not see, but it is somewhere that enjoys the taste. This somewhere is evidently the inner side of the self. Based on the provision of the received dreams, the inner side is the product of the interaction between the organism and the environment; it is alive but invisible; it is always moving; there is no abiding inner side; it is the bearer of the phenomena, a kind of ground for the outer half of the self; it takes a picture of every object seen; it supplies the outer half with the energy it needs; and it lights up the outer half thus making it visible.

In a way, the view expressed by Pierre Jean Cabanis in the 18th century regarding sensation seems to agree well with our dreams regarding the origin of the inner half of the self. Cabanis said, "Sensation (consciousness) is a relationship between the organism and the object, resulting in a conscious condition."[7]

The received dreams that substantiate the above statements are numerous. Here are some examples:

- *You are located in a spot that no one can see you.*
- *The outer two (the organism and the environment) send forth the inner counterpart.*
- *The inner side subsists on the feed sent from out there.*
- *The inner side is alive and capable of seeing.*

- *The dark, inner side is always on the move.*
- *Like an invisible bird, the inner side is at different places at different times.*
- *The inner side is something like a magnetic field.*
- *The inner side, like a bridge, conjoins the organism and the environment.*
- *The inner side unites the separate parts of the outer half.*
- *The inner is the bearer of the outer phenomena.*
- *The inner side, like a camera, takes pictures of the outside world.*
- *The inner is the process of picture-taking and memory-forming.*
- *The inner provides energy for the outer half.*
- *The inner side is the discoverer of the outer side.*
- *The inner side, like a search light, lights up the outer side.*
- *The inner side makes organism and environment visible.*
- *The inner side consists of relatedness and connectivity.*
- *The inner side is a form of distillate of the outer side.*

The Outer Side of the Self

It was discussed earlier that the organism and the environment give rise to the inner side of the self through their interaction. These two elements are physical; they function involuntarily or unconsciously. As Richard Bently said, "Matter has no life or perception and is not conscious of its own existence." The inner side is the aware or conscious side but is invisible; hence we generally know nothing about its content. This problem is remedied by the outer side of the self, namely, by realizing the fact that the outer side is actually a detailed presentation of the inner side. Things that have gone into the inner side have equipped it with the power to reflect them into the objective world, thus producing diversity and multplicity. The outer side of the self not only provides a footing or grip for the inner, but it also reveals in a most concrete manner what the inner contains or of which it is made up. Only particulars can specify what the universals are. The organism and the environment beget universals which are unmanifest; the objects seen or conceived identify the content of the inner side of the self, thus making the unknown known. We cannot have a conception of the innner side without the outer side. The latter is the exemplification of the former.

The above proposition is expressed by our received dreams thus:

- *The outer keeps the inner alive moment by moment.*
- *The outer is the objectification of the inner.*
- *The outer consists of objects that name the inner.*
- *The outer is a showing of the inner.*
- *The outer is the multiplicity of the inner unity.*
- *The name of what is in this dark inner space is expressed in what is out there.*
- *The outer is a mirror in which the face of the inner appears.*
- *The outer functions as the language of the inner.*
- *The outer can be described as adjectives qualifying the inner.*
- *The outer is the identifier of the inner.*
- *As a section of a tree identifies the age of a tree, the outer identifies the nature of the self.*
- *The outer is the detailed copy of the inner.*
- *The outer is the measure of the content of the inner.*
- *The proper designation for the outer side of the self is dead material. Yet it provides all the feed the inner side needs.*

Hegel's standpoint seemed to be in line with the position of the above dreams when he said, "The nature of spirit may be understood by contrasting it with its opposite, namely matter."[8]

Our dreams also describe the outer side of the self as a vehicle for the inner. Here are some samples of such dreams:

- *The physical side of the self carries the non-physical side.*
- *The outer side functions as a vehicle for the inner.*
- *There is a car that carries you around.*
- *Consider the outer side as a sort of conveyor for the inner side.*

Self as One which is Two

Self is a union of two halves of two elements in one reality, which is the act of seeing. The inner half and the outer half are distinct from the standpoint of visibility, sentience, and constitution, yet they are complimentary. They are inseparable so much so that one cannot exist without the other. The motion or interaction inherent in the gerund "seeing" encompasses both halves of the self. According to the dicta of the received dreams, the self is a unity derived from duality.

Dreams specifying the nature of the self as unity in duality are worded thus:

- *Self is one thing but includes what is above and what is under.*
- *Self comprises the invisible as well as the visible.*
- *Seeing conjoins the inner and the outer half of the self.*
- *Seeing consists of what is visible and what invisible. Seeing incorporates what is on both sides.*
- *Seeing is unitary because it contains its content.*
- *The self feeds on what is on its both sides.*
- *Self as seeing includes the dark side as well as the bright side.*
- *The self as seeing comprises two elements: a live element and a dead element.*
- *The inner and the outer dyad are not two independent units, they form one integrated whole.*

It appears that the concept of the unitary self is represented adequently by the model of the self, Figure 1. The top part or the inner self of the model (N) expresses a floating field. It consists of interaction, motion, relationships or a coming all together. It is a unity, since seeing is inclusive of its content (D or K and L). The organism and the object are manifestations of what is unmanifest. However, the organism and the environment or the object are not aware that they are part of the inner, united half. Individuals see themselves separate or independent from the inner half, yet, unbeknownst to them, they exist because they are connected to the inner half, which is the source of their lives. Thus, it seems that the self floats between the inner and the outer half by its motion; it connects and enfolds both sides, thus producing unity.

Summary

The self has been equated by other writers with such terms as mind, soul, spirit, psyche, ego, I, knower, etc. For all these terms, our received dreams mainly used either consciousness or the gerund seeing. The latter term is used more often due to the fact that is it a gerund, a verb. Seeing as used by our dreams covers all mental activities, but also the seen as discussed in Chapter 2. The main emphasis of our dreams is that the self is a verb, a process, a motion, not something static with fixed boundaries. To be seeing necessitates the presence of two objects, an individual through whom seeing can occur and a piece of the objective world, capable of reflecting its images. The outer half of the self or the two objects produce the inner half. The self as the act of seeing constantly moves or interacts between its two halves and as a result, the unity of the self is achieved.

Figure 1 shows how self as seeing operates. The function of the inner side of the self, which is invisible and lies in a field above the organism and the environment is to make the outer half visible, to take the picture of the object seen, and to supply energy for the outer half. The function of the outer half of the self which consists of both the organism and the environment is to show the content of the invisible side of the self. In a way, the outer half is made up of the details of what is unmanifest. It qualifies as well as identifies what goes on within us at any given moment. However, according to our dreams only the inner half of the self is living; the outer half is dead. In some respect, the self model is like the working of the Tao in the Chinese philosophy. The two sides of the Tao, the dark and the bright, operate together in a creative process.

The striking features of the model self as unity are its transitoriness and its fluctuating boundary. The content of the self shifts and becomes something different with every object observed, and the boundary of the self as seeing extends beyond the individual and ends where the object is located. Obviously the individual is an important element in the threefold structure of the self, but it is a zero without a figure in the absence of the outer world and the interaction inherent in seeing. Therefore, based on the content of the current chapter, the definition given for the self in chapter two as the self can be amplified to read: Self, as "I am that I am" has an inner side and an outer side, which constantly interact with each other and thus produce consciousness, or seeing, through their motion.

Chapter 4

The Self as Transcendency

I am a part of all I have met.

~Alfred Tennyson

If you go throughout the length and the breadth of the universe, saying I include this, I include that, so that nothing is left that is not you, then that you are.

~Huston Smith

IN THE PREVIOUS chapters, it was discussed that the self as consciousness or seeing is a verb, a process, or motion. It is not a thing with fixed boundaries situated in a particular location in our body. If the self has no specific locus, how could we find out about its nature or structure? This chapter aims at answering this question based on the provisions of the received dreams. The gist of what is going to be presented is that we as selves or as seeing entities are not in our bodies alone. In addition to our bodies, that bit of objective world that we see or think about at each instant is part of us. This implies that the self has a transcendent character. It goes beyond the limits of the skin and extends above and beyond the body. As Bergson has remarked, "In perception, we are actually placed outside of ourselves."[1]

The received dreams seem to highlight the transcendency of the self on three bases.

1. Object as part of the self
2. Past as part of the present

3. Unity inherent in the self

Object as Part of the Self

We have already noted on several occasions that the act of seeing must pass from the subject or agent to an object or a patient, otherwise no seeing, no consciousness, or self is tenable or knowable. Self as seeing knows itself as it "goes beyond" itself; there it finds an object that at that moment complements the self and due to this complementing or due to this outer half, the self becomes aware of itself or finds existence as well as an identity. Without an object to see, no self, no identity will come to light. Since the object that the self sees is in the outer half of the self, the inner half of the self must always transcend or traverse to reach it. Our dreams make it clear that the self or seeing is not something inhabiting in the so-called fistful of quivering meat that is commonly known as brain or the center of consciousness. To use Carnap's phraseology, "I (self) is like an unending surface in space; it does not fill space and yet unlike triangles has no boundaries."[2]

As discussed in the preceding chapter, the process involved in the emergence of the self runs something like this: first the person and the object that the person sees give rise to the inner half of the self; then the inner half spontaneously contacts its source, its outer half. As a result of this up and down movement, the self eventuates. The point is that this up and down movement cannot occur within the body. We must transcend the body and reach at different points of the external world at different points of time so that the self comes about and continues to expand. Wittgenstein said; "The limit of language means the limits of my world." Our received dreams seem to say that the limits of my seeing are the limits of my world.

The theme of chapter 2 was "I am that I am" or the self as seeing is that which it sees at any moment. It was emphasized that as we see *that* we become conscious and find the self moment by moment, or one might say as we become aware of that which is there our inner self comes into being. When there is no object, there is no seeing, and when there is no seeing, no self is in existence. Our received dreams used the pronoun "that" to refer to our own bodies too. In other words, all the visible things we see become the constituents of our inner halves, of course, one at a time. The important point is that in all cases there is a considerable physical distance between the inner half that sees and the outer half that, from the standpoint of the structure of the self, does not see but makes the inner half seeing. To cover this distance, the inner self must traverse or transcend as far as the actual location of the object. If the object is the moon, the inner self has to traverse as far as the moon so as to be able to appropriate it, making it part of the whole self. From this standpoint, one might say the universe is more myself than my particular body.

As Byron's Corsair sings:

O'er the glad waters of the deep blue sea,
Our thoughts as boundless, our hearts as free.

The view that we, as seeing beings, are in a real sense the outer world, is not something new. That man was the universe in miniature was clearly expressed by the Greeks. Anaxagoras spoke of all things in all. Protagoras insisted that man is the measure of all things; of that which is that it is and of that which is not that it is not.[3] According to Plato, man is in touch with the whole universe through his soul. For the Zen Buddhists, there is no duality between the self and the external world. Everything is included within the self or man. Also in mysticism others become identical with the self. Pure consciousness or the self is the principle of all that exists. Mahmud Shabisteri, the 13th century Sufi, sung of man's status thus: "The world has become man and man has become the world. In no better words can man's dignity be put forth." Overall, most mystics believe literally everything is in everything.

Among those in the West who have expounded the thesis that the self extends beyond itself is Alan Watts. In several works, he kept stressing this belief. In one book, he observed: "Self is far beyond the image of ego or of the human body as limited by the skin. We...behold the self wherever we look and its image is the universe."[4] In another work, he writes: "There is no self without...other, no matter how separated this other may be. But standing in the way of this recognition is the fear of finding out this external world may be only oneself.[5] (When we realize our true nature,) we find ourselves not in a world but as a world...."[6] In another passage, he questions: "How many of us now realize that space is the same thing as mind or consciousness that when you look out into infinity, you are looking at yourself, that your inside goes with your entire outside as your front with your back, that this galaxy and other galaxies are just as much yours as your heart and brain"… "Thus, the universe is more yourself than your particular bodies."

Along the same line, in 1936, Edmund Husserl declared the transcendental ego to be correlative to the world. He explained: "Once we perform the reduction, we discover whatever is in the world is only an object for our pure consciousness."[7] In the same vein Royce pointed out, "The world and the mind are organically related; neither can be taken apart from the other; there can be no object without a subject that knows it."[8] Finally, physicists Seeley and Baker hold that "consciousness is fundamental reality…that in actuality, we are all one, not many, a single cosmic mind."[9]

The received dreams first stress that we are "that which we see there;" then point out that to reach "that which we see there" requires that we "go beyond" that part of the self which is unmanifest but is capable of seeing. Hence in every instant of seeing, the inner half of the self must transcend. The following dreams should shed more light on what was just said above:

- *You are a seeing being.*
- *That which sees is not a thing.*
- *Your dwelling is really in your seeing.*
- *As you see various physical objects, you, as a seeing being, become those objects.*
- *All that you see is in effect your outer half.*
- *If you are those which you see then you have always to travel a distance to reach them.*
- *Self as seeing extends as far as its objects are located.*
- *Self is transcendental.*
- *The objects seen are the limits of transcendental self.*
- *You are always on the go. You come from there and go back there while alive.*
- *To be a self involves being in possession of something from outside.*
- *When the inside goes outside, the outside comes inside.*

- *The outer world is reference of the inner world.*
- *You are the real world.*
- *If you are that which you see, it means you have had to transcend with every object you have seen.*

Past as Part of the Present

According to the received dreams, the self as seeing or as consciousness has two modes from the standpoint of time: consciousness of the present and consciousness of the past; or the self as a conscious being is the child of the past as well as the present. In general, consciousness always represents the "now moment"-awareness of something. Even the past has to become present to be noticed. In a way, the self as seeing is like a river, we move along and become renewed with every encounter we have with bits and pieces of the outer world, and everything we see or encounter remains with us. In a special sense, we carry all we have seen or experienced, and one way to know who we are is to recall where we have been at any point of time and what has been our interaction with those that had presence for us. The outer world we have gone through reports eloquently on the kind of life we have lived. The places we have been, the people we have met, the words exchanged between them and us; all have had a part in laying the foundation of the self.

The formal psychology deals extensively with the functions of memory. Retention, recall, recognition, retrieval, types of memory, and functions affecting memory have all been studied, analyzed, and reported extensively. Particularly, great attention has been given to the part that the brain plays in retention and recall. Also various models of memory have been proposed from the notion of impressions made on brain tissue, from B.F. Skinner to more recent developments concerning information processing or the formation of neural groups. The cortex is thought, by some theorists, to be the site of the brain's memory function. Also some believe that the reticular formation is the location where our mental capacities are situated. Others have asserted that we are, in a sense, our reticular formations or our brains. However, as yet, no general agreement has been reached concerning the nature and locus of memory. Our knowledge of brain physiology has increased immensely, but we still have scant knowledge of the nature of memory.

It was mentioned earlier that the self also consists of the "now moment" as well as all the now moments of the past, which are generally referred to as memory. It was also indicated that in order for the self to exist there must always be three elements present, namely; the inner half, the outer half and the interaction between the two. This seems rather obvious in conjunction of the ongoing now moments. When we consider the past now moments, the concept becomes rather hazy. To say that we all now carry within ourselves what we have seen in the past or we retain what has given rise to our identity seems unnatural or absurd. What we need to remember is that we are exploring the nature of the self not that of the organism bound by the skin. The self as a seeing entity is subjected to a different set of rules.

In this connection, we should not lose sight of the "I am that I am" principle. We acquire an inner world because there is an outer world. We have an inner half—a mind, or thinking, sensing, seeing abilities—because there is a world with physical features, which enables the inner half to take a picture of them and retain them. We always carry this picture with us, and because of them, we can maintain our sanity and identity. However, these pictures are different from ordinary ones; namely, they must always appear in pairs. Not only must we have a copy of past physical objects, but their originals (the material from which the copy is made) must also be coupled with it; otherwise, we would lead a life like those suffering from Alzheimer's disease. We would see the picture but make no connection.

How our selves can become carriers of both pictures and originals, our received dreams do not specify, but in the context of the transcendental self and the fact that the skin is not the limit of the self, the answer may be that we as self are vast beyond measure. We seem to extend as far as our seeing, thinking, or imagination can take us.

The main reason for including the topic of memory in support of the transcendency of the self is the fact that the past does not really pass away. While we live, we are in a way the bearers of our pasts. If memory consists of the past now-moments of seeing and if seeing must always contain its objects to remain seeing, then I, as self, must be the storage of all objects I have encountered in life. This means the past subsists in us not only in the form of an image; the past is alive with all concrete objects that have gone into the making of the act of seeing.

Thus all objects we have crossed in the past must have presence for us all the time so that our memory remains functional, or we would not be able to maintain our sanity. In Alzheimer's disease, the connection with the objective world through which we have gone breaks down. We see our dad or a picture of him, but we can no longer recognize him. This happens because our seeing or our recognition loses its contact with the object it used to have. The object is no longer part of the triad of the "subject-object-interaction." It was mentioned in the preceding chapter that in the absence of any of these three elements, seeing cannot take shape.

The idealist Bishop Berkeley claimed that the tree we see is in our mind. Bertrand Russell maintained that only the picture of the tree is in our mind. Our received dreams seem to side with Berkeley as in the act of seeing or knowing, the subject cannot materialize without the presence of those pieces of real world that were the objects of our seeing. Consequently, if objects such as trees, mountains, and people have been parts of our selves in the past, they are parts of us currently or while we live. From this point of view we can say we are definitely much vaster than the confines of our skins. We are transcendental indeed as we are all that we see now and all we have been seeing in the past, if our memories are intact and active.

The received dreams do not present the topic of transcendency involved in the self the way that was outlined above, but they bring the concept to notice pithily. Here are some specimens of the dreams touching upon memory dynamic and transcendency.

- *The past is the sum of now-moments.*
- *The past is now present.*
- *You always live in the present moment.*
- *If there is something that you carry with you, it must be reckoned as your reality.*
- *You are a kind of conveyor belt, carrying material stuff that has given rise to your inner side.*
- *The relation between the two sides of you can be explained by this dialogue: the inner side tells the outer side, "You bring the outside world inside me so that I become your carrier." The outer side responds, "Of course."*

- *If everything is an experience we carry them because of these experiences.*
- *Self as seeing flows like a river.*
- *Self becomes renewed with every encounter it has with a new object.*
- *The outer half of the self is a well-kept record of your inner half.*
- *Your inner half comes into existence as a result of all the places where you have lived or stayed.*
- *To a degree, you are made up of all the locations that have been once your domicile.*
- *If you want to know who you are you should take into account every object and place that has served as a building block of your inner world.*
- *The objects you have seen are the records of your being.*
- *Now-moments make up the past.*
- *The places where you had residence determine the quality of your inner side.*
- *Losing touch with the outer world where you once lived is tantamount to losing your sanity, as the inner depends on the outer for nourishment.*
- *The outer as object gives rise to the inner as subject.*
- *At every instant that you see an object, in a way that object gets attached to you.*
- *Like a bird that, once it sees something sticks to it and will not let go, when you see an object, you also somehow retain it.*

Unity Inherent in the Self

People raised in Western cultures generally believe that the self is in the body. It is somewhere beneath the dome of the skull or somewhere in the brain. The received dreams specify that we are not in the body alone, but because we are seeing entities or conscious individuals, our substance is really outside the body. That which is outside our body gives rise to our consciousness, our mind or the inner half of the self. Long ago Plato reminded us that the body itself never has knowledge. The word existence or exist (ex – out + sister – to be located) implies what is known by the inner half of us, are things in front of us. The self as transcendency means going beyond or exceeding limits of the skin and by such acts, the inner half finds content. As a result of this transcendency, this up and down motion, the inner and the outer halves of the self become united and function as a well-coordinated whole; therefore, the whole self as seeing becomes a bridge between the inner half of the self and the outer half.

Many philosophers have expressed the view that the subject and the object are one. Specifically, Aristotle remarked, "That which knows and that which is known are really the same thing,"[10] but apparently by subject they all refer to the mind of the individual within the skin. Our received dreams ascribe awareness to the inner half of the self which underlies the individual and the object. When our dreams refer to the unity of the subject and the object, they refer to the unity of three elements: 1) a subjective side that is capable of seeing, thinking, and knowing; 2) an objective side made up of the individual and the object and 3) the interaction that constantly occurs between the two sides. In this context, the meaning of transcendence approximates that of the interaction.

As discussed in chapter 3, what makes for unity of the self is motion, interaction or what has been referred to by our received dreams as a "verb," and presumably the gerund seeing has been substituted for consciousness due to its verbal character. From our discussion so far it is evident that seeing as a verb is a unity. The motion, the flux, the interaction involved in the transitive verb expresses the fact that one activity, one process is at work at any instance of seeing. The gerund seeing is unity because it is always inclusive of the seer and the seen; knowing is unity because there must be a knower and a thing to be known in order to materialize. Beating is real if there is a subject and an object, a beater and a beaten. The gerund seeing, knowing, beating, etc. cannot occur in a vacuum. They are always associated with an agent and a patient as well as an operation, a dynamic or activity that connects the two. Thus, according to our dreams and Figure 1, when the self as seeing goes up, it gives rise to the seer and when it comes down to the seen. This means the seer and the seen both become parts of the up and down motion. Consequently, motion and duality establish unity. We and others become one at every junction of seeing, and the oneness thus expressed seems to agree with the views of some physicists who propose the interconnectedness of all things. On the absolute oneness of things, Fritjof Capra wrote:

"The principal school of Eastern mysticism…agrees with the view of the bootstrap philosophy (originated with physicist Geoffrey Chew) that the universe is an interconnected whole, in which no part is any more fundamental than the other so that the properties of any one part is determined by the others. In that sense, we can say every part contains all the others…."[11]

Similarly, Plotinus observes: "All are mirrored in everything. One sees all in the every other."[12]

One of the most important questions in philosophy and physics concerns the nature of reality. Some physicists have declared that consciousness is necessary to create reality. Our dreams seem to indicate that reality comes into existence as the self carries out its transcendental function. Idealists hold that reality is to be found in an idea. Our received dreams seem to say reality is to be found in the self as a seeing or transcending entity. This implies that self or reality is a kind of interaction or relationship between the inner and the outer worlds, a relationship that makes for unity. Our dreams specify that "self and reality are one" and to know self is to know reality, and self as seeing is unity.

Descartes divides the world into two separate sorts of reality: the reality of consciousness and the reality of matter. According to him, the self becomes the pure subject for whom the world is object. The dicta of our dreams indicate that self as seeing is the one thing with two sides: an evident side and a hidden side. This means both evident and hidden are seeing which is a unity. Dreams that refer to the unity of the self or seeing are numerous. Here is a sample of them:

- *Say seeing comprises both in and out.*
- *One is the inner self and the outer self.*
- *The inner and the outer selves both are parts of seeing.*
- *Seeing occurs due to its dark and bright side.*
- *The inner and the outer are attachments of the self.*
- *The overlying and underlying make up one through their interaction.*
- *You are both subject and object.*

- *You are a dynamic entity. When you go up, you become invisible; when you come down, you become visible.*
- *You move constantly between up and down and as you do so, up and down become parts of you.*
- *In fact, you are the bearer of both this and that.*
- *You tuck in what is on both sides.*
- *You are holders of two worlds.*
- *In every particle there are the properties of all other particles.*
- *The self establishes unity out of duality.*
- *As self, we see everything as one.*
- *Know seeing is one.*
- *It is obvious that the self is unity of myriad objects.*

The necessary consequence of the above dreams is the transcendency of the self. If the inner side of the self and its outer side are united through their interaction, it implies that interaction is the connective that brings about unity, and interaction involves transcendency.

Summary

From the time of the early Greek philosophers, when referring to the self their reference in general was human beings confined within the outer covering of the body. The received dreams consider the self, which only humans possess, is equivalent to consciousness or seeing in its broadest sense. The model of the self, Figure 1, shows that the self is dynamic and its essence is motion or interaction. This means that the self is transcendental; it goes beyond the limits that conventional beliefs have assigned to the body. The interaction between the organism and the environment (both of which lack the power of seeing) give rise to the inner half of the self, which has the capacity for seeing. Then the inner half interacts with its outer half, making it visible. Based on the received dreams, the self is this interaction, which at all times is linked on the one side to the visible outer half and on the other to the invisible inner half. The activity, thus ensuing indicates that self is transcendental, and the individual as organism is only one element of the triad that constitutes the self.

It was also discussed that memory is a good testimony for transcendency. If we have to know ourselves and remain sane and fully functioning, we must not only have a good picture of the details of the past events of our lives, but also we must perceive and recognize at present the actual person, place, and events that we have encountered. It seems as though our selves somehow should constantly in physical form carry all things experienced or known by it in the past. Based on the understanding we have of our dreams, what enables the self to have such capacity is the connectivity that results from its transcendental nature. In massive amnesia, the person simply wanders aimlessly about and forgets who he is or where he is because the connection with physical details of the subject's past life, probably due to intolerable stress, breaks up. In such cases, the self loses its transcendent property. It was also indicated that the self is a unity in duality. Such unity involves rising above or going beyond the limits of the organism or the environment.

To expand the definition of the self once more, our dreams tell us that in addition to being that which we see at any moment and to being a motion, we are also transcendent. If we want to know who we are, we must, in a sense, carry with us all the objects we have seen or experienced in life; otherwise we cannot claim to possess an identity nor can we maintain our sanity.

Chapter 5

The Self's Similitude to the Deity

The knowledge of the self is the basis of our knowledge of God.

-Hugh of St. Victor

Without God, the vast universe is devoid of meaning.

-William Earnest Hocking

Man has been created in the image of God.

~ Genesis 1:26

IN THE PRECEDING chapter, it was stated that the self is as vast as the world we experience. Does this mean each one of us is all that there is as some solipsists have claimed, and there is nothing else beyond us or beyond the observed world? The answer, according to the received dreams is a negative. There is something else, something that most people believe in, yet they do not know what it is. Almost one half of the received dreams deal with the existence of the Deity and its nature. Initially, it must be mentioned that the descriptions of the Divine by some philosophers are notoriously difficult to relate to the empirical facts of life. Furthermore, some say our knowledge of the Divine is always inadequate since as soon as we go to describe the transcendental nature of Him, we are forced to speak in a metaphor or an analogy that has been used in common language, which is ruefully unsuited for the purpose.

On the other hand, we have philosophers like Hocking who says:

"God has something to do with the meaning of things....The world is alive with meaning. Without God...the vast universe is devoid of meaning. With God, the world has sense, perhaps a direction."[1]

Or the English novelist and socialist, H.G. Wells remarks:

"Until a man has found God and been found by God, he begins at no beginning, he works to no end."

As we glance about curiously at different segments of the world we find order, harmony, unity, beauty, and purpose. If this is true, there must also be an orderer, harmonizer, unifier, beautifier, and a purpose-assigner. These signs are evident wherever we look. Hence, this wonderful fabric of the universe cannot be the work of chance. An underlying eternal author must be at work to set things in proper shape.

Many terms have been used by different thinkers to identify this eternal author. It is called "God" by English-speaking believers, the Absolute One by Parmenides, "the Supreme Good" by Plato, "the Pure Act and First Mover" by Aristotle, "Cosmic Reason" or Logos by the Stoics, "The Wholly Other" by some Jewish theologians, the "Unity of All Life" by Augustine, "The One" by Plotinus, "Everything that truly is" by Erigena, "Nature" or the world by Spinoza, "Pure Mind" by Ibn Sina (Avicenno), "Supermind" by Berkeley, "Infinite Mind" by Kant, "Everlasting now" by Carlyle, "Supera Consciousness" by Bergson, "Being" by Eckhart and St. Thomas Aquinas, "the Absolute Being" by Cabalists and Husserl, "All inclusive reality" by Hegel, Bradley and Bosanquet, "the Being of being" and "ground of reality" by Heidegger, "the Ultimate ground of being" by Tillich, "infinite consciousness" in Hinduism, "Supreme reason" by Brightman, "Supreme Self" by Royce, "Overself" by Emerson, "Self of the World" by Alan Watts, "The Eternal Presence" by Martin Buber, "Principle of Concretion" by Whitehead and "The Ultimate Secret of Reality" as used in one of the received dreams. In keeping with wording used by our received dreams, we generally use the familiar terms God, deity or divine throughout the text.

How can we gain some knowledge about this eternal supreme source known as God? Many philosophers including Kant have said it is not possible for humans to fathom into the mystery of the Divine through arguments, logic, or didactics. He is an ineffable and absolute mystery. Whitehead remarked, "You can argue to doomsday as to whether God exists or not, you will not prove anything…"[2] To Whitehead, God is self-evident. The view of the author of this work is that the Divine is self-evident at least through two channels, through our dreams and through observing our own physiological constitution.

Based on the message of the received dreams, it is clear that the Divine himself is the author of the dreams of every dreamer. He seems to use dreams as carriers of messages that can lead to self-knowledge and to better understand the reality of the Divine. Rahner said, "God is who God reveals God to be." Accordingly, dreams are perhaps the most dependable form of verity, regarding the nature of human and divine. One of my dreams runs in these words: why do we dream? To understand our Divine source.

Dreams are revelations, the best of its kind. One of the most basic thoughts in the early history of the Greeks was that dreams come from a reality outside the rational, from empirical dreamers, a source beyond the reach of senses. This external source was punctuated by the use of the wording "seeing" a dream rather than having a dream. There is also considerable evidence that the Divine, at times, has revealed Himself to a number of those chosen through mediums other than dreams, but the dream medium is open to almost every individual every night, and when understood, dreams can impact the dreamer more deeply than other mediums since they emerge from within oneself.

The fact that the dream phenomenon happens regularly teaching us something that we have never heard of before and is coherent, consistent, and meaningful over a considerable span of time all indicates a supreme intelligent author is behind the dreams. Soon it becomes evident to us that this author, in order to let us see that which lets itself to be seen, makes full use of our total capacities so as to go beyond the discursive level of communication. According to Thomas F. O'Dea, "The history of the Hebrews and of the Christian Church from this point of view seems as the unfolding of a dialogue between God and man."[3] This author must admit that what he has learned from his received dreams, a small portion of which are reflected in this book, has almost all been new to him, despite the fact that he has been in one way or another a student for all of his life.

Why do many people not dream or why do people not remember their dreams? Perhaps the answer is the dreamers' belief systems and their physical conditions. If they believe that paying attention to their dreams is meaningless and a waste of time, they obviously show no interest in their dreams and often ignore them. These individuals seem to find some sufficient ground for ignoring their dreams since, as mentioned in chapter 1, almost all dreams, at least initially, are in an inscrutable code. Furthermore, the physical condition has something to do with dreaming and recalling dreams. If we are overly tired or have not had enough sleep or have had difficulty falling asleep these could very well have a negative impact on us. In general, it seems that we dream less when we are in the state of deep sleep and more when drowsing or snoozing. We also assume that other factors are involved in this process, the examination of which is beyond the scope of this chapter.

Another simple proof for the existence of the Divine, besides volumes of material written throughout history by others on this subject, is the fascinating way in which a host of systems in our own bodies function. Our most immediately important system is that of the respiratory. An average adult breathes more than 12,000 quarts of air a day. With the oxygen that we receive, we burn food and release energy. Our hearts beat about 70 times a minute and pump 4,000 gallons of blood a day. Our digestive system has a mechanism for propelling the food along its course and see to it that every part of the body gets, for growth, its share of nutrients of the right kind, in the right amount and at the right time. Our nervous system, including our brain, which is made of billions of neurons, regulates hundreds of activities such as our heart beats and mediates messages that move our muscular system. Scores of other less well-known systems are at work to keep the body healthy, well-fed, and well-balanced. Overall, it seems the parts and functions of the organism contribute to the welfare of the whole and appear to realize specific ends.

Nothing can approach the complexities and tantalizing processes involved in the multifarious systems with which our body structures are endowed. What is so obvious about these systems is that all of them are spontaneous or automatic. They are not entrusted to our wits. We have nothing to do with their designs and their operations. If we decide to stop the air from entering our lungs, we cannot do so for more than a minute or two. If we, as individuals, have no part in manipulating what goes on in these systems, if everything in the body works independently of what we think or do, if these systems which are mindless or unconscious in themselves and are unable to decide about their own operation, and if no actions happen without an actuator, then all that takes place within our skins must have a source other than ourselves.

The operation of systems of such high excellence needs a coordinator of superior intelligence, knowledge and purpose, who can uniformly coordinate the functioning of all the bodily systems of every individual from the fetus stage to the last days of life. How can all these marvelous chains of operations be random? It is said that nature takes care of all that which happens. This view can be accepted if nature is endowed with intelligence and purpose. Then nature will be close to what the received dreams reveal about the reality of the Divine.

In this connection the words of Thomas Aquinas are apt.

> "Natural bodies act as if guided toward a definite goal or end so as to obtain the best result. This fitting of means to ends implies intention. But seeing as natural bodies lack consciousness, they cannot supply the intention themselves. Therefore, some intelligent being exists by whom all natural things are directed to their ends; and this being, we call God."[4]

Along the same line, C. Lloyd Morgan observes that there is evidence of purpose everywhere, and this is due to the creative and directive power of God, which is immanent or indwelling in every one of the multitudinous entities that make up the whole. The above remarks are close to the worldview of a good many idealists, who believe that all space and energy, solidity, and motion of matter is the functioning of God or some mind.[5] The idealists are not the only group who have such beliefs. Any sensible individual knows that physical things do not think nor do they have knowledge of ends.

If we accept there is a deity in the world, how can we know Him? According to our received dreams, the most effective way to know the

Divine nature is self-knowledge. This is the topic we take up in the following section.

Human-Divine Connaturality

According to our dreams, self-knowledge is the royal gate to the knowledge of the Divine. There is connaturality between our essence and His. In the 12th century, Hugh of St. Victor remarked that the knowledge of the self is the basis of our knowledge of God. In the tradition of Islam, there is a saying that unambiguously declares: "He who knows who he is, verily he also knows who God is." The passage in the Bible (Genesis 1:20) says that God created Adam "in our image, after our likeness" has been recognized by some church fathers as an ideal to be strived after by the faithful. Some have specified when we realize our true self, we find ourselves one with Him.[6]

To see God in the human image is objectionable when we have a false image of ourselves. When the concept we have of the self is limited to the skin which physically separates us from the rest of the world, then we cannot conceive any affinity to the Divine. French philosopher Michel Montaigne said, "It is not an insult to God but the very reverse to ascribe to Him attributes, which are also characteristics of humans."[7] It is also stated that Plato sought to raise the human spirit into a likeness with God. Locke presented this likeness in a different way. He pointed out that: "All events have causes; hence, they resemble their cause."[8]

Our dreams reveal that we are akin to the Divine as well as parts of Him. Here are some specimens of received dreams which specify that humans are clues to knowing the nature of the Divine.

- *The self of humans is the secrets of my being.*
- *I am like you.*
- *God and human nature are the same.*
- *Man and God are alike.*
- *Humans are the children of the Divine, so they are like their father.*
- *You are like myself.*
- *The fact that you understand the words used in your dreams shows the presence of connaturality.*
- *Humans are the secrets of the Divine.*
- *Man is like God.*

Therefore, in order to know God, we must first know ourselves. As we gain a better understanding of our own reality, we learn more about the reality of the Divine. This does not imply that we will fully comprehend the mystery of His existence. Probably, our knowledge of Him will always remain incomplete.

According to the received dreams, the human and the Divine have at least the following seven characteristics in common with each other:

1. Both denote being.
2. Both represent activity.
3. Both signify seeing.
4. Both are inclusive of concrete reality.
5. Both imply dipolarity.
6. Both express unity.
7. Both show intelligence.

Both Denote Being

It is self-evident that we as humans exist both in the form of mind or thought as well as matter or physical objects as discussed in chapter 3. Likewise, based on the testimony of the received dreams, the Divine exists and the word "Being" is used to affirm His existence as an actuality. A number of philosophers have also referred to the Divine as a Being. Philo of Alexandria said God is "*to on*" that which is, par excellence, and this being is rather the most universal of all. The famous Catholic theologian, St. Augustine held that "pure being in general" is expressive of God. Also Eckhart remarked that God is "being per se" or all that is. He emphasized that all beings including the human soul are none other than God. Specifically, Thomas Aquinas believed that God is "Being in itself."[9]

Some of the dreams that explicitly punctuate that God can be denoted as being are:

*   *Clue to God is being.*
*   *God is being.*
*   *Whatever form of being exists that is God's being.*
*   *I am being.*

- *See me as being.*
- *Being is God's being.*
- *God is the whole being.*

The fact that the Divine communicates with us in our dreams and we have the experience of becoming his communicatees indicates not only that we have the quality or state of existing but as noted earlier, we are connatural with Him.

Both Represent Activity

Again we learn from our dreams that the being of humans and the Divine are a special kind of being. It is a being that always moves, interacts or acts and reacts. In other words, both are of a dynamic nature; both are a process activity or a verb. In the Bible, we read "...the Word was God." (John 1:1) The term "Word" comes from the Latin *verbum*, or verb, and a verb indicates what somebody or something does or what is becoming of something or somebody. So "the Word was God" could very well mean verb or activity or motion is the nature of God. This seems to correspond with Aristotle's position when he declared God was pure action. In chapter 3, it was also remarked that the nature of the human consists of motion or activity. The dreams quoted before and the dreams quoted below all indicate that the nature of the Divine, similar to that of the human; is something like motion or activity.

The following dreams confirm this concept.

- *I am a verb.*
- *A verb is my whole being.*
- *We are a kind of verb that takes two objects.*
- *When you refer to my existence as God, you should think of something dynamic.*
- *A verb is all I.*
- *Affirm that the essence of the Divine is activity.*

Both Signify "Seeing"

If God is being per se, what can prove His "beingness" or His state of existence? As discussed in the preceding chapter, what makes it evident that something exists is the gerund seeing when seeing is considered as a blanket term for sensing, thinking, experiencing, or consciousness in general. Seeing or consciousness encompasses and makes known all that exists, and according to the received dreams, the verbal noun seeing is a proper route to conceptualizing the Divine.

Some well-known thinkers have referred to God as consciousness. Aristotle defined God as pure thought (which is a mode of consciousness). Also the Upanishads stress that the essence of Brahman is pure consciousness. Hegel uses the term "reason" instead of consciousness to refer to the Universe. The Divine is described as Omni-Consciousness by Alan Watts and as Consciousness by physicist Amit Goswami. Perhaps it is not a coincidence that the ancient hieroglyphic for God was the figure of an Eye upon a scepter to denote that he sees or is conscious of everything. Our received dreams use the verbal noun "seeing" to define the nature of the human and the Divine.

In the preceding two chapters, it was discussed more than once that the essence of the self is consciousness or seeing. Our dreams also specify that the same can be ascribed to the reality of the Divine. It is well to consider that in Hebrew God is referred to as "el ro' i," the God who sees or sees me. The following received dreams are very explicit in this regard.

- *I am my seeing.*
- *All is seeing.*
- *Seeing is God.*
- *All being is seeing.*
- *Call seeing as God.*
- *We are nothing other than seeing.*
- *Know all of I is seeing.*
- *The nature of God is seeing.*
- *I is just seeing.*
- *I am a seeing being.*
- *Whatever is, is seeing.*
- *Seeing is inclusive of all being.*
- *All that exists is seeing.*

In some dreams, consciousness has been used instead of seeing. It was hinted that the two terms have been used interchangeably by received dreams.

- *Say I am consciousness.*
- *Say God's being is consciousness.*
- *All of I is consciousness.*
- *Consciousness is the essence of the Divine.*
- *Being is consciousness*

Both are Inclusive of Concrete Reality

In chapter 2, it was explained that the best way that the self can be defined is to consider the content of seeing at any given moment. If we see or think of a beautiful object, at that moment, our inner self will consist of beauty, and vice-versa, if we see or think of an ugly sight our inner existence, at that instant, will be nothing other than ugliness. In short, we as selves, are that which we see or think at any moment. As we shall see in the next chapter, the same thing that was said about humans regarding the constitution of the self applies to the Divine's nature also. The phrase in the Bible "I am that I am" seems to apply equally to humans and to God. Since this will be discussed at length in the next chapter, we will quote here only a few dreams that make a reference to this topic and perhaps shed some light on it.

- *Say I am that I am.*
- *Say that I am the real world.*
- *What you see there engenders what is here.*
- *The concrete side of the world gives rise to my creative side.*
- *The make-up of my inner world is derived from the real world.*
- *Know my "I" here is my "me" there.*
- *That which is evident shows my hidden side.*

Does the foregoing smack of pantheism? The answer is both yes and no. It is pantheism since our received dreams specify that God is one and one is all. Pantheism, as formulated by Spinoza in the 17th century, holds that God and Nature are two names for one reality. From one perspective, this is analogous with what our dreams have revealed. However, as it will become evident in the next chapter, our received dreams' positions are based on the nature of the Divine as a seeing being or consciousness. Seeing is a unity made up of the subject and the object and the interaction between them. Based on this explanation the nature of the human and the Divine is alike; we humans as selves or seeing beings are "that which we see." The Divine likewise is "that which He sees." In this sense, the translation of the tetragrammaton transliterated, YHWH as "I am that I am," expresses best the reality of the Divine. Thus, from the standpoint of pantheism, the view of Spinoza and that of our dreams seem the same.

Both Imply Dipolarity

In chapter 3, it was discussed that the self has two sides, an inner side that is conscious but featureless and an outer side that is unconscious but featured. Our dreams tell us that the same dipolar character is true of the Divine also. After all, God must have some feature so that He can see and know Himself and can realistically be known to humans. If the world we have gone through was not provided with form and lineament we could not develop a mind and become conscious of ourselves. Logically, the same applies to the Divine. If He is conscious, His consciousness must have content, and content must consist of a real, featured, concrete world. Again, we defer further elaboration of this topic to the next chapter. What we need to say about the similitude of the Divine and humans is that both have a manifest side and an unmanifest side, and the following dreams attest to the dipolarity inherent in the Divine.

- *Say that I have an inner side which serves as a container and an outer side which is the content.*
- *That which is there not only is there but also here.*
- *I am the inner as well as the outer.*
- *If there is an external world then there must also be an internal world.*
- *If something is seen there, something must be here that does the seeing.*
- *See I have a side which is unity and a side which is multiplicity.*
- *I am both the evident and the hidden.*

Both Express Unity

In the preceding section, it was mentioned that the Divine has two sides, a non-material side that sees, knows, or is consciousness, and a material side or a physical world that is seen by the first. As discussed before many philosophers including Descartes had difficulty in this regard. He considered mind as one kind of substance and matter as another kind. Hence, he thought that they could not act upon each other. Spinoza solved this problem of bifurcation by declaring that there was only one thing, and that was God; mind and matter were the two aspects of God's unity. What our received dreams say in this connection is in some respects closer to Spinoza's position. Our dreams tell us that the inner and the outer, the unmanifest and the manifest, the conscious and the unconscious side came into being as a result of the interaction which occurs constantly between the two sides, and this interaction leads to seeing, which is a unifier.

The gerund "seeing" that is used to characterize both humans and the Divine needs to be amplified again. Logically, there can be no seer without a concrete object to be seen, and likewise there will be no object, no "seen," without a seer. What brings the seer and the seen together is the act of seeing which results from the interaction between the seer and the seen. The act of seeing, when it materializes, not only substantiates the seer and the seen but also brings about unity.

Perhaps the concept we are considering can be expressed best by an analogy. A man may claim "I am a lover," without having any particular person in mind. A woman may make a similar claim saying, "I am beloved" without having a lover. Obviously the statement on the part of both is absurd. Their statements will become meaningful if some form of expression of love between the two actually occurs. In this example, although, three elements are involved—a lover, a beloved and the interaction between them—in effect, loving materializes only if three elements are combined. Similarly unity inherent in the self and the Divine arises from the conjunction of the seer, the seen, and the act of seeing. We can also say unity results from the interaction between the subject (the seer) and the object (the seen). My dreams refer to the matter in either way.

The Persian poet and mystic Abu Said expressed this unity in a dialogue between man and God thus:

Man asks God: "Who art thou with such splendid beauty?"

God replies: "I am unity or you might say totality.
I am the lover, I am the loved, as well as loving.
I am the mirror, I am the face as well as the seeing."

My dreams on the subject of oneness and unity of the Divine are multitudinous. The following is a sample of such dreams.

- *It is unity which brings to pass the subject and the object.*
- *God is the unity of all things.*
- *There is oneness in the universe.*
- *See! All is one.*
- *God and man both are unity.*
- *Remember seeing make for oneness.*
- *You can say being is one and one is I.*
- *Know God's being as the one.*
- *Know consciousness as the one.*
- *Call me as unitary consciousness.*
- *The basis of the Divine unity is the unity of consciousness. Consciousness in all of its aspects is one thing.*
- *Whatever is visible is the secret of the one.*
- *Say the one is God*

Some other received dreams that attest further that the Divine is all and all is one. Here are some examples of such dreams:

- *Say all is I and all is seeing.*
- *See me as all.*
- *See God is all.*
- *I am all being.*
- *Know the whole is I.*
- *Know I is totality.*
- *I contain all the world.*
- *Say all is one and all are in me.*
- *One way to express my allness would be to say the following:*
- *I means God*
- *Thou means God*

- *He/she means God*
- *We means God*
- *You means God*
- *They means God*
- *All means God.*

Both Show Intelligence

We should have no doubt about the presence of intelligence in human beings. The entire history of mankind in spite of its setbacks and shortcomings is rife with discovery, development, and invention. Pascal said, "Man is a reed, but he is a thinking reed." Descartes, after all his search for finding who he was, came to the conclusion that he was a "thinking being." He had doubt about the existence of his body but not about his mind as a thinking entity. Generally, when we think, we use or exercise our mind to create or devise something or solve a problem. One might say all thinkers are intelligent people. Because of their intelligence, they reveal good judgment and sound comprehensive thought and often create or invent new devices, objects, ideas, or procedures that make life easier or achieve lofty purposes.

We should not forget that many of the important inventions were adopted in pre-historic time. Those people were intelligent enough to develop tools to cultivate plants, domesticate animals, devise building techniques, produce and control fire and invent the wheel and much more. The present era of history has occurred with phenomenal developments and inventions in all fields of human endeavor. Realistically, there have been thousands of inventions and discoveries since the machine age, covering practically all fields and areas including transportation, business, medicine, industry, communication, recreation, space exploration and molecular biology. Progress in so many varied and complex fields is a good testimony to the fact that humans possess and show supreme intelligence, originality, and resourcefulness.

Likewise, nature is indeed the work of a supreme genius. All things in the universe that are not made and operated by humans and are spread before our view are a kind of beauty, craftsmanship, and splendor that defies description. In all of them, there is a signature of wisdom, power, and ingenuity. All celestial bodies, animals, humans and plants follow lawful, predictable courses. All is managed and conducted with perfect frugality and efficiency. The sight of the immense galaxies, of clustering stars and of deep blue sky are so overpowering that the vision of them brings a great sense of awe. Approximately, 30,000 kinds of fish are known, each with its special hues and patterns. A number of tropical fish, notably the butterfly fish, are extraordinarily impressive with their beauty. Their coloration strikingly serves as camouflage.

In the physiology of humans and other animals, all systems function uniformly, each equipped with mechanisms geared to accept nutrients that are suitable, reject those that unsuitable, and carry all functions in harmony and communicate with other systems. In the plant world, a grain thrown into the ground unfailingly brings forth crops and fruit in due time, and trees of the same species produce and shed leaves always as they did before. A vital question remains: does the sky, the fish, the body, the grain, the tree decide when to operate, how to operate, and what effects to produce, or is there a motivating, guiding force behind each. Our received dreams' answers are the latter.

As said earlier, it is obvious that an intelligent and wise power or force coordinates all these phenomena and the continuity of their functions. If the laws of nature are the rules according to which things operate, there must be a rational, purposeful lawgiver. As a matter of fact, the elegance, grandeur, and resplendence characteristic of various parts of nature shine so brilliantly that one can hardly doubt the existence of a masterful, purposive, intelligent being, who has everything well in hand. Things in nature do not stand on their own feet, nor do they have the ability to think. The curious reader may ask why we have not included any dreams on the topic of intelligence of humans and the Divine. The truth of the matter is that we had no dreams precisely specific on the topic of intelligence, presumably because the matter is self-evident.

Summary

In this chapter an attempt was made to give an outline of what the received dreams have imparted about the nature of the Divine based on the postulate that the Divine and humans have certain characteristics in common. Conjecturing and speculating with regard to the existence and the reality of the Divine have been the perennial quest of philosophers and theologians throughout the history of thought. What was presented here was not based on the speculation or presupposition of the author or other writers but was based primarily on specific messages revealed by the received dreams which specify that the nature of God and that of humans are alike. Dreams containing these messages were classified under seven heads as follows: first, humans and the Divine are both *beings* existing as actualities in time and space; second, humans and the Divine are both *dynamic* processes or marked by continuous activity. Their structures are set up like a verb, a motion, not something fixed or static; third, humans and the Divine both can be characterized as consciousness, but since consciousness is a noun, our dreams have substituted seeing for consciousness to stress the active quality present in both; fourth, "I am that I am" applies to both the identity of humans and the Divine both consisting of that which they see. The object they see moment by moment constitutes their seeing, hence their beings; fifth, both are *dipolar*, the human and the Divine both have two sides, one is visible and the other invisible; sixth, the two sides of humans and the Divine form a *unity*. In both cases, motion or interaction unify the visible and invisible sides. Seventh, being a seeing entity, both humans and the Divine possess reason and intelligence. In the case of humans this is evident from all that they have invented, discovered and achieved thus far. This is much more evident with respect to the creative ability of the Divine. When we consider the evolution and all the developments that have occurred since the beginning we find ample signs of the Divine's intelligence. The fundamental component subsisting in the similitude between humans and the Divine appears to be the verb "seeing" that subsumes all the common characteristics mentioned above.

Chapter 6

The Deity as I am that I am

...God said unto Moses: "I am that I am."

-Exodus 3:14

Man must learn to recognize the sign of God in the sign of the universe.

-Aristotle

"The world determines God; God determines the world."

-Alfred Whitehead

IN THE FOREGOING chapter, our discussion concentrated on similarities between the nature of the human self and that of the Divine. We concluded if we really know who we are, we will find good clues as to who He is. This chapter is concerned with inherent or distinctive characteristics of the Divine with specific reference to the Biblical ascription of the Divine as "I am that I am" (Exod. 3:13).

According to the Bible, the words exchanged between Moses and God run thus:

> "And Moses said unto God, Behold, when I come unto the children of Israel, and shall say unto them, the God of your fathers hath sent me unto you; and they shall say to me, what is his name? What shall I say unto them? And God said unto Moses, "I am that I am": and he said, thus shalt thou say unto the children of Israel, I AM has sent me unto you..."

As shall be seen later in this chapter, the above wording of the Divine's name is in accord with thousands of messages received through our dreams, regarding the identity or the name of the Divine. The basis for justifying such name or attribution for the Divine is the fact that He is essentially of the nature of verb (word) or activity, and the verb form that characterizes Him is seeing as discussed in the previous chapter. Seeing, which is used as a substitute for consciousness, will materialize only if there is an object to be seen, an object that can produce seeing. Hence, in the ascription of "I am that I am" there is an "I am" that does seeing and an "I am" or a physical world, that produces seeing. Thus the two components are one. Some of the dreams that confirm this statement are:

- *Know God is of the nature of consciousness.*
- *You can say all is seeing instead of consciousness.*
- *"I" is all seeing.*
- *Seeing needs form in order to actualize.*
- *Seeing has always a concrete component.*
- *Activity is my nature.*
- *I am a verb.*
- *I am seeing.*

More dreams will be quoted later to substantiate the fact that God as a seeing entity always needs a phenomenal world as the feed for the existence of its ultra dimensional half. In short, God said to Moses if the children of Israel want to know me all they have to do is to see me there. What is there is my content and what is here is the container for that which is there.

Two Phases of the Divine

The foregoing remarks indicate that, like the structure of the self, the Divine has two phases or two dimensions, namely, visible and invisible or immanent and transcendent. Our received dreams specify that the Divine has a side which is alive, conscious, capable of thinking and creating and a side which is dead, unconscious or bland, yet this very same side is the begetter of the live side. In many religions a sharp distinction is made between the world and the Divine. Our dreams present both as two aspects of one unity. In some respects, the position of our dreams is similar to that of Plato who believed in a divine soul and a divine body and to that of Spinoza who maintained the nature of God is thought as well as extension or is something unmanifest and something manifest.

In fact, Spinoza restated in different context what Galen said in the second century AD that mind and matter are different aspects of the same stuff. Plato emphasized that the universe was the divine body and held that this body was in the Divine soul, not separate from it. According to Plato, God is bound on the one hand by the world of forms and on the other by matter. Alfred Whitehead referred to the dipolar nature of God thus, "The world determines God. God, of course, determines the world by His completion of it." This seems to bear affinity with the verse John 1:1 "The Word was with God and God with the Word" when the word is taken to mean God's creative activity, especially as manifested in the creation and preservation of the world. Dreams referring to the dipolar nature of the Divine are many. Examples of such dreams are:

- *I am both soul and body.*
- *I am both subject and object.*
- *I am the inner reality and the outer reality.*
- *I am evident and hidden.*
- *I am the name and the named.*
- *One half of my being is internal, the other external.*
- *My external part is the world.*
- *The outer half of me is dead but not the inner half.*
- *What is standing there is the inner side of me also.*
- *My inner side is one, my outer side many.*
- *I am more than the sum of objects present in the physical world*

The above dreams show clearly that the Divine is a whole or totality, which is a composite of a physical side and a non-physical side.

How could the two-fold nature of the Divine be put into a form that helps visualize Him or enhance greater understanding of Him? As discussed in chapter 3, our dreams have presented us with a diagram that was displayed on page 52. This author has had some difficulty in describing certain features of it, but overall it has shed considerable light on the rather complex concept of the Divine. The diagram, in a crude way, is analogous to a half spherical bowl turned upside down. The inside of the bowl is dark or invisible, but the outside of it is visible in the light since the bowl is placed on a surface made of glass that reflects what is inside the bowl. Thus the upper part of the bowl represents the inner half of the Divine, and the lower part with the glass surface, is the outer half. The Divine as a seeing entity is the composite of the two halves as well as the force behind their operation. (See Figure 2)

The Divine as the Unity of Two Phases

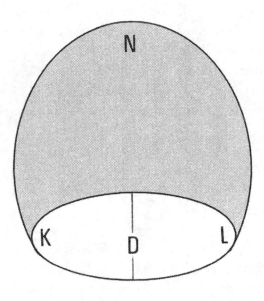

Figure 2: Shows the two phases of the Divine making up His whole identity.

Figure 2 shows that the Divine is not a static entity. He is of the nature of seeing, and seeing involves movement. The two phases on the physical side of the Divine (K and L or temporal and spatial) are like two mirrors in front of a black hole that reflects the content of the black hole moment by moment. Unity is characteristic of this process. The visible or manifest side issues the invisible or unmanifest side and the latter side projects the former. In fact, as noted earlier, our dreams specify that the visible side is dead; life inheres only in the inner the side of the Divine. Nonetheless, the content of the inner side is derived from the outer side. As such, the inner side always contains or encloses the outer side. Thus the Divine can rightfully utter "I am that I am since that which is in the physical world makes up the content of my non-physical side.

As observed in conjunction with human identity in chapter 3, the essence of the self was presented as un-deux or a one which is two. The same principle seems to apply to the nature of the Divine. A large number of our dreams specify that the Divine is an entity that can be characterized as un-deux (one-two in French), un or N representing the inner half of the Divine and deux (D) representing, the spatial, temporal half of the Divine. Together they form a unity. The following dreams punctuate that it is the unity-in-duality that makes up the structure of the Divine nature:

- *You can say I am two-ness. (I am duality.)*
- *I am really two.*
- *See that God is being un-deux (one-two).*
- *Consciousness is my essence.*
- *Say the two (spatial and temporal) make up my consciousness.*
- *The two define my oneness.*
- *Say God one is God two.*
- *Being I is made up of that side which is two.*
- *The side which is two (my physical make-up) is one with my non-physical make-up.*
- *Each instance of the one comprises the two.*
- *My subjective side which is unitary embodies my objective twin side.*
- *You can say my side which is two gives rise to the side which is one.*
- *See me as a being which consists of two beings.*
- *Affirm that there is no God other than God who is unity in duality.*

The invisible side of the Divine that animates, unifies, sees, knows, and sets in motion all things in the visible world is described by our received dreams as follows:

- *My invisible side is the conscious side of me.*
- *My invisible side is the locus for thinking and knowing.*
- *My invisible side is unity.*
- *My inner side embodies all that is in the physical world.*
- *My inner side is composed of my outer dyad.*

- *My inner side is comprises all that is in my visible side.*
- *My outer half describes my inner half.*
- *My inner side is formless.*
- *My invisible side brings the visible side to light.*
- *My invisible side is indeed my aware side.*

Some thinkers have expressed the view that the universe of matter is the body of God, but most religions make a distinction between God and the world. For instance, Carl Barth said, "God is in heaven, man is on earth." Our dreams see God and the world as one but they stress that God has two dimensions or two aspects, the inner and the outer, as noted earlier. The dreams quoted above described the nature of the inner side of the Divine; the dreams listed below are portrayals of the outer side of the Divine:

- *All that is visible is the front of what is in the back.*
- *What is evident shows what is hidden.*
- *What is manifest is my concrete side.*
- *What you see is a showing of my inner side.*
- *Every corner of the physical world reveals the form of my inner side.*
- *My outer side is virtually dead.*
- *Things in my manifest side comprise the particulars.*
- *The visible world is my speech.*
- *My manifest side is my expounder and my exemplifier.*
- *Objects seen in the physical world need to be taken as my names.*
- *My outer side speaks of my history.*
- *The outer side is the secret of my seeing.*
- *The outer side is the clue to my inner world.*
- *The outer side and the inner side function as one unit.*
- *What you see there is a presentation of my subjective side.*
- *My manifest side produces content for my unmanifest side.*
- *The manifest side shows my physical features.*

It was pointed out that the essence of the Divine being is seeing, and seeing occurs when the two sides interact and bring about unity moment by moment. Thus the act of seeing overcomes the duality of the seer and seen or the knower and the known by encompassing both, as was the case in reference to the self of humans. Here are some dreams confirming that the Divine as seeing is the unity of His manifest and unmanifest realms.

- *Seeing is the conjunction of what is evident and what is hidden.*
- *Say that the invisible and visible are one being.*
- *The Divine is both the container and the content.*
- *I am out there as well as in here.*
- *There and here are one.*
- *In and out lead to unity.*
- *Under and over make one.*
- *I am a totality which is made up of that which is within and that which is without.*
- *I am one as well as many.*
- *I convert one into many and many into one.*
- *The inner and the outer are components of my seeing.*
- *Seeing is unitary.*

How could two things, the inner and the outer sides of the Divine, be explained as one? One answer is that each side is itself as well as the other. Using our notations, N is N as well as D and D is D as well as N. The other answer is that the unmanifest side in a sense enfolds the manifest side, and seeing which is the nature of the Divine materializes if there is a seer and a seen interacting with each other. The following received dreams seem to confirm what was just stated:

- *What is here is me as well as that which is there.*
- *My manifest side is my manifest side as well as my unmanifest side.*
- *That which is my outer half is there as well as here.*
- *The seen is the seen as well as the seer.*
- *The whole outer world is inside me.*
- *My inner side is the holder (or the bearer) of the outer side.*
- *All that which constitutes here is all that which constitutes there.*
- *My inner being consists of that which is there.*
- *Consider my unmanifest side to be a container for the manifest side.*
- *There is one substance but it is made up of two kinds of things.*

- *That part of me which is physical is also non-physical.*
- *The inner and the outer are constituents of seeing.*

God as I am that I am

We have come in a roundabout way to the main topic of this chapter, namely, to the conclusion that the phraseology "I am that I am" is a proper name for the Divine. How can this be explained or supported? The answer again is in the nature of the gerund "seeing," to which we have already reverted in several places. Seeing, knowing, and other related synonyms can take place only if there is something to be seen or to be known. Without a seen or a known, seeing or knowing is inconceivable. In other words, there can be no subject without an object and there can be no object without a subject or some mind to be aware of it.

Realists argue that there are myriads of objects in the world without the presence of a witness or a knower. Although such a statement is valid per se, it is invalid from the standpoint of the seeing or knowing of a particular individual or a conscious entity. Seeing, knowing, being conscious must have content and the content must be an object existing in the concrete world. Additionally, objects can give rise to subjects and subjects to objects only if they interact with each other and that which makes the interaction or the union between the two sides possible is the "verb" seeing, which is the essence of being, reality, or God.

Based on what was said above, applying the name "I am that I am" to the Divine seems perfect. The Divine is a seeing being, and as a seeing being, He must have two sides, a side that can see and a side that can provide content for his seeing. Hence, the Divine says to Moses, I, as a seeing being, consists of all that which is there or all that which makes my seeing hence my being. In other words the Lord says I am the entire concrete world that produces my inner half. The postulate "I am that I am" comprises the bulk of our received dreams both in conjunction with the human and the Divine. Here we quote a small number of such dreams or messages, appertaining to the Divine, which are specific enough to convey what was just said:

- *I am the seeing of my other side.*
- *What is there is me.*

- *Seeing means I have the knowledge of what exists there.*
- *All I is the seen.*
- *I am my objective side.*
- *That which is there is my secret.*
- *What is there is my identity.*
- *Say the I is me.*
- *I am that which is in my concrete side.*
- *What is manifest represents I.*
- *All that which is there is all that which is here.*
- *What is manifest corresponds to my unmanifest side.*
- *All that is there is a reflection of my being.*
- *All that exists there is the content of my being.*
- *That which is manifest is my name.*
- *My inner side is the ground of my outer side.*

The pronoun *that* in the phraseology "I am that I am" stands for the generic term that stands for a person, place, thing, idea, state, event, time, remark etc., supposed to be understood by the party present. In conjunction with the Divine's identity it stands for all that is visible and has concrete form. The problem of the identity of the Divine is fundamental. Based on our dreams what identifies the Divine is "*that*" which serves as a referent. God must have a referent to be known. Without a referent what is said about Him in order to identify Him will be more like fantasy than real. The name "I am that I am" puts an end to fantasizing. The Divine becomes as real as any concrete object that we see here. The following dreams stress that the whole concrete world reveals the Divine's identity or everything becomes an attribute of Him.

- *That is my whole I.D*
- *That reveals the real side of me.*
- *That shows my form at any moment.*
- *The manifest world is my referent.*
- *That is the secret of my being.*
- *That says who I am.*
- *That is really my name.*
- *That also reveals my history.*

- *That is, in a way, my picture.*
- *That shows what is here.*
- *That is indeed my face.*

The pronoun *that* is used in the construction of "I am that I am" apparently comprises two counterparts, namely space and time. Like the model of the self (Figure 1: page 53) that has a physical side made up of organism and environment; similarly, the Divine's constitution has two counterparts in His physical side. These are presumed to be space and time or extension and duration. Thus everything that happens in the external side of the Divine has a spatial or temporal dimension as Figure 2 shows. The view expressed here is akin to what Hegel said that the Absolute Spirit reveals itself through spatial and temporal creations.[1] Likewise, Samuel Alexander believed that space and time are stuff of which things are made.[2] Specimens of dreams that speak of the spatial and temporal aspects of the Divine are;

- *My outer side is a dyad consisting of temporal and spatial realities.*
- *Space and time are the extensions of my entire being.*
- *Space and time are my manifest half.*
- *Space and time serve like two legs on which I stand.*
- *Space and time are two forms of mass.*
- *My non-physical half is made up of two kinds of mass.*
- *My spatial and temporal side gives birth to my non-physical side.*
- *All that you experience in the spatial and temporal world bespeak that you are experiencing me.*

Meanwhile, my dreams seem, in a way, to lend some support to the doctrine of the Trinity in Christianity. According to the scriptural testimony, there are three distinct persons in God: the Father, the Son, and the Holy Spirit. This is, in some respects, close to what was called earlier here as unity in duality. If we consider the Father as the unmanifest subjective side of the Divine and the Son as the manifest objective side of the Divine and the Holy Spirit as the verb "seeing" which serves as a conjunction between the two sides, then we have a unity in duality or a

Godhead made up of a society of its two divine halves. Our dreams bear considerable testimony to the formulation just stated:

- *The hidden side of the Divine is the Father, the manifest side is the Son.*
- *The son comprises all the physical world.*
- *All consists both of the father and the son.*
- *The father and the son are God's referents.*
- *I am the father as well as the son.*
- *I am the synthesis of the father and the son.*
- *See the Divine as the father as well as the son.*

Working out the Father-Son relationship in ontological terms is never easy, but considering the Divine as the eternal seeing or consciousness makes it rather comprehensible to think of Him as a being with a subjective side (the Father) and an objective side (the Son) and as a verb or a process (the Holy Spirit) conjoining the two sides. We should recall John 1:1 that says "...the Word was God" and the Latin for "word" is verb, activity, or process. For the purposes of our dreams the word is seeing, which is inclusive of the seer and the seen or the internal and external worlds.

Summary

This chapter considered the question of the Divine's identity based on the Biblical wording "I am that I am." This phraseology has been interpreted differently by different theologians. Apparently, no author seems to have taken it in its straight-forward sense that our received dreams' messages clearly import. According to the dreams, the Divine nature is what grammatically can be called a "verb" or activity. The verb adopted by our dreams to express the Divine's nature is seeing—seeing equivalent to consciousness. Consequently, the first thing, significant about the Divine's nature as seeing is its need for an object. There is no seeing if there is nothing to be seen, and if nothing is there, nothing can be here.

Accordingly, if the Divine is an entity with the power of seeing or consciousness, He must have two sides or two natures: an inner side, which is invisible but does the seeing or is conscious, and an outer side, which is visible and provides content for the inner side but lacks consciousness.

Hence, the phraseology "I am that I am" is a concise affirmation of the premise "what is there is me." I need a reference; what is there is my referent. More precisely, I am the totality resulting from the interaction of my two sides. According to our dreams there is an interchange by which the objective side creates the subjective side, and the latter creates the former. The outer side is a galaxy of objects, all of which reveal the names or the attributes of the Divine. The inner side unifies, enfolds, and actuates all that is there. Of preeminent significance is the fact that the inner side and the outer side are two complementary correlates of one single seeing being who encompasses all and is in motion all of the time, and it is presumed that in some respect, the above characterization of the Divine coincides with the Christian doctrine of the Trinity.

Chapter 7

Self as Deity

The good consists in mystic union with God.

~Spinoza

You are always united with the Lord, but you must know it.

~The Upanishads

READERS WHO HAVE followed our presentation thus far should have a good idea that our dreams speak of two types of self: a self that is confined within the skin and a self that has no boundary. Perhaps a better term to call the first is ego and the term "Self" proper to be reserved for the type without boundary. What was discussed in chapter two by psychologists and others was mainly an exposition on ego or the usual self concept that almost all people have of themselves. Our dreams' depictions of the self are totally different from all that has been said about ego or from the image nearly all of us have of ourselves. Making a distinction between these two types of self is of fundamental importance. Hence, they need to be elaborated further.

To fully understand the difference between the two types of self, we must have a good picture of how each develops. To present, the development of our usual self concept, we must go to the time that a baby is born. The newborn virtually has no mind or no concept of itself. It is only the seat of life but with tremendous abilities or potential to see what goes on in the environment, to record and store what it sees and hears, and above all to register its response in contacts with its caregivers and others. These events happen to it, so to speak, without its permission. At the early stage of life, the baby is totally receptive. Later it may exhibit resistance in some situations. Presumably, this is partly due to its constitution, but mainly it is due to what it has learned and experienced earlier.

The experience of the young child forms the concept of his reality. The child sees the world the way he has gone through it. He relates to himself and others based on what he has experienced. The contacts he has had, the words he has heard, the scenes he has seen, the feelings he has had in every situation all afford him a sense or a perspective as to what is real and what is unreal, what is right and what is wrong. Thus he develops a unique way of viewing or judging things. This unique way of seeing the world has been called by different terms including, outlook, worldview, viewpoint, belief system, frame of mind, and more. Perhaps a more suitable name would be: "The determiner of future course of life." No doubt cultural mores, lures, and opportunities also, to a degree, play a part in giving form to the development of the child. The problem about this sense of reality is its permanency; what one experiences in childhood almost always irrevocably seals one's fate.

Many of the things we have been taught are fictitious or apocryphal. If, based on the feedback we have received, we have come to believe that ghosts are real, this concept of reality makes us avoid any place that has been declared haunted. If authority figures have convinced us killing others by setting off an explosive bomb and committing suicide will take us directly to paradise, we act upon this concept of reality that we have inherited from the culture in which we were born. Hundreds of such examples can be cited, but, the limits of this chapter prevent more from being listed.

We have been told everywhere—at home, in school, by parents, teachers, psychologists and philosophers—that we, as self, as conscious beings, are separate from others. This has been considered as a truism, as something too obvious to even mention since the body of each individual stands apart from that of all others. Superficially, this truism is accurate. For practical purposes, this separateness is necessary. It must be observed and respected so that the criteria and limits of social relationships and individuals' private lives can be established. What is inaccurate is that we, as self, are confined within our bodies. There are whole areas of the self that are beyond our bodies. In reality, that which explains our thoughts or behavior is not our physical make up; it is our psyche or what our dreams refer to as "self," which include the body. It is said that Descartes on the basis of three dreams arrived at his well-known *cognito ergo sum*, "I think, therefore I am." He defined man as a thing which thinks. In his meditation, he expressed a doubt whether there are "sky, air, earth, colors, shapes, sounds or any existence at all but inventions of my mind."

As discussed in the second part of chapter 2, the true nature of the self is consciousness or seeing, and consciousness or seeing actualize due to the presence of an objective, physical, or material world. If the essence of our being is thought, consciousness or seeing such being needs content. As discussed profusely earlier we are that which we see or, stated differently, the content of our thoughts or seeing really owns us. In essence, that which we see there, or that which we think, at any moment, expresses our beings more meaningfully than our bodies do.

Repeating the principle "I am that I am," our received dreams tell us that we are much more than our bodies; we are connected to others and this connection is as vital as the connection we have with the air we breathe. As there will be no life, if there is no air, so there will be no seeing, no thought, no intelligence, no mind, and no self if there are no others. Alan Watts expressed our problem in this area as the following:

> "The nub problem is the self-contradictory definition of man himself as a separate and independent being in the world."[1]

> "The most strongly enforced of all taboos is the taboo against knowing who or what you really are behind the mask of your apparent separate independent and isolated ego. Under such conditioning, it seems impossible and even absurd to realize that myself does not reside in the drop alone, but in the whole surge of energy which ranges from the galaxies to the nuclear fields in my body."[2]

At the beginning of this chapter, it was indicated that there are two types of self: a self whose boundary is the skin and which is considered to be separate from others and a self without boundary, which conceives itself to be actually connected with others and all concrete phenomena. Our dreams consider the latter type of the self to be part of deity. The self as part of the deity will be treated in the next chapter. In the rest of this chapter, we quote and examine dreams that deal with the divine nature of the self in general. As we shall see later, humans are humans not only because they are similar in nature to the Divine but also because they depend on Him for survival. Whether we see ourselves as beings separate from Him or united with Him, in either case, we are not self-sufficient, self-regulating, or self-existent systems. We depend on our beyond for every breath and for every instance of remaining consciousness.

The belief that we are God or parts of God has been held by many thinkers, saints and sages since the dawn of civilization. In Greek philosophy, Pythagoras and Empedocles claimed to be gods. Also Socrates considered the self to be transcendental. He thought of the self in a sense as divine; thus, he saw divine elements in all beings. In particular, the orphic Plato and Stoics regarded the human soul to be part of the deity. The view that by knowing oneself, we learn to know God and to be known by Him so as to be deified is also expressed by orthodox Christians as well as by some who are non-orthodox. Paul's words in Acts are: "For in Him we live, and move and have our being" (Acts 17:28). The sixth verse of the eighty-second Psalm reads "I have said: You are Gods and all of you are children of the Most High." Also, St. Paul remarked: "The spirit is primarily the divine element in man." Moreover, in first Corinthians, we find these words: "He that is joined unto the Lord is one spirit with Him" (1 Cor. 6:17). Unfortunately, the idea of being identical or united with God has been strongly opposed by theistic religions. It is condemned as pantheistic and blasphemous.

Philo of Alexandria (15/10 BC – 45/50 AD) who is considered the most important representative of Hellenistic Judaism and a forerunner of Christian theology, held that man is akin to the Divine and has unbroken access to it from within. For him, intellect is an impression of the Divine being, a ray of the Divine light, or a fragment of the Divine being. Egyptian-Roman philosopher Plotinus (205-270 AD), the founder of Neoplatonism, declared: "To acquire identity with the Divine is the most positive of all conditions in life. In such a state, we melt to a oneness with the Absolute, wherein no shade of difference enters...."[3]

Another new Platonist who believed in the identity of man with God was John the Scot to whose name sometimes is added "Erigena." He held that "the creature is not distinct from God. The creature subsists in God and God manifests Himself in the creature in an ineffable manner."[4] The philosopher who was more emphatic in this connection is the Dutch Jewish philosopher Baruch Spinoza (1632-1677). He claimed that "man arises in God and lives in God, and it is in this very concrete sense that he himself is divine…."[5]

The spiritual quest for union with the Divine is the goal of mysticism, some form of which is found in all religions. In Christianity, the theme of union with the Divine has appeared in the writings of St. Augustine, St. Teresa of Avila, Meister Eckhart, and his 14th century successors. Eckhart was almost certain that the soul is the same as God. In Hinduism, one can realize true identity only through identification with the Universal Self. The Indian philosopher and theologian Shankara said: "Bliss means the realization of one's identity with the Divine." The Upanishads says "He who knows Brahman becomes Brahman, and to become one with Him is the only wisdom." To the Indian, it is clear that the self is not different from God, and that so far as a man is in the self, he is not only contained in God but actually is God.[6]

In the West, Ralph Waldo Emerson repeatedly asserted the unity of all individual souls with one another and with God. Also Josiah Royce, an American philosopher who taught a monistic idealism, maintained that each individual is a unique phase of the divine life.[7] By the same token, Carl Jung, who considered the concept of self beyond comprehension, concluded: "It might equally well be called the God within us." Finally, the Nobel prize winner, Austrian physicist, Erwin Schroedinger, commented on Leibniz's doctrine of monads: "All of us living beings belong together inasmuch as we are all in reality sides or aspects of one single being, which perhaps in Western terminology is called God, while in the Upanishads, its name is Brahman."[8] In sum, what was said above seems to point to the position of our received dreams that we are all one with the Divine.

Deity of the Self based on the Received Dreams

In this section we deal with the theme of the divinity of the self on the strength of a large number of received dreams. More than what was said so far, these dreams testify to the divinity of humans, justifying it at least in three different ways:

1. Pronouncing direct messages.
2. Equating God with all existence.
3. Equating self with seeing.

Pronouncing Direct Messages

Messages that specifically state that the self is divine are multifold and multiform. In view of the preeminence of their significance, we quote a relatively large number of them below:

- *Call yourself as a being who sees God.*
- *Those who become awake will realize that their identity comprises me.*
- *If my being is inside your being you are the bearer of my identity.*
- *If that which you carry at every instant is me, you are nothing but me.*
- *If all that operates in your system is my energy, how can you call yourself to be independent of me?*
- *As you learn that my outer half (physical world) is the creator of your self, then you really know who you are.*
- *You acquire my identity the moment you experience me inside yourself.*
- *As the content of your being is my being.* You must always identify with me.
- *The measure of your real being is the degree in which you come into possession of my being.*
- *I (God) really own all of you.*
- *When, through seeing, you attach to yourself a part of me, you consist of that part of me.*
- *If my presence be absent in you, you really cannot exist.*
- *It is my being that makes you conscious.*
- *The energy at work within you all comes from me.*

The following dreams are even more unequivocal and clear-cut than the ones just quoted.

- *Man is God.*
- *God you are as you are.*
- *Know thou art I.*
- *You are my very self.*
- *Your identity is that of mine.*
- *When you want to think of yourself, think of me; not yourself.*
- *I is all of you.*
- *I is your being.*
- *God includes all.*

Equating God with All Existence

Unity of all things is the doctrine of most Eastern philosophers, and it is found in Hinduism, stoicism, idealism, and mysticism. Modern physicists also speak of the interrelation and interdependence of all things as well as the basic oneness of the universe. This indicates that one force, one energy pervades everything. Scientists use the general term "nature" to refer to this force. Our dreams seem to be in accord with Spinoza, who formulated the most thoroughly pantheistic system, believing God and Nature are one; they are two names for one reality.

The major difference between the worldviews of the scientist on the one hand and our dreams and pantheism on the other is the presence of an overall intelligent coordinator who encompasses everything. The great majority of scientists do not believe in any supernatural phenomena. Hence they must attribute the intelligence governing natural force to matter. In their view, for example, the earth decides to orbit the sun at the speed of 18.5 miles per second, completing its rotation in 365.25 days.

The emphasis of our dreams is that God is all of the existence. This stance, in some respect, is akin to monism, which avoids making a radical distinction between the Creator and His creations and which explains all that exists in terms of a single reality. The upshot of it all is that if God is all that exists; humans, ipso facto, become parts of Him—a subject which will be discussed in the following chapter. The question that legitimately arises is this: If God is everything that exists, then criminals, wrong-doers, villains as well as virtuous individuals are all representations of or the manifestation of God Himself.

Based on our understanding of the received dreams, good and evil, miseries and felicities, all represent the Divine's actions. Things that seem evil or painful are considered necessary because they challenge us to grow by facing and overcoming them so that the trend of evolution may continue. However, this is not a proper place to say more on this subject. We must return to our main theme, which is God is all that exists, and we are gods simply because He is All.

Below is listed a sample of dreams that specifically speak of God as all, as one, or the unity of all things:

- *Unity of all things is God.*
- *God is equivalent with unity.*
- *See all things as God.*
- *See me as all.*
- *The whole existence is I.*
- *I am the totality of all things.*
- *I am the sum of all things.*
- *All being is my being.*
- *See all being is one and I am the one.*
- *I contain the outer world.*
- *The whole being represents me.*
- *I am consciousness and consciousness is one.*
- *See the universe as oneness.*
- *All that you see is my face, and my face is your face, too.*
- *The United State is literally God.*

Equating Self with Seeing

In chapter 5, it was pointed out that humans and the Divine are connatural. In chapter 3, it was shown that the self as seeing has an inner and outer side. The two sides with their interaction make up the total self. Thus, based on the principle "I am that which I see" elaborated on in chapter 2, if the inner, subjective side of the self sees that which is in front of it is God, the inner self in the same breath becomes God since the inner self is the container of the outer self. In a word, seeing things as the manifest side of God makes the "self" God. We used the quotation mark for the word self to re-emphasize that the concept of the self as revealed by our dreams is different from the self concept that we have been taught or from the picture that we have of ourselves as a bunch of bones and flesh within skin.

As indicated earlier, everyone knowingly or unknowingly is God or parts of Him because God is all-inclusive and because what everyone sees at any instant is the manifest side of God, but to fully realize the status of Godhood calls for intentionality. Attention, when directed to an object, says that object must be viewed as a piece of the Divine. Those who do not allow themselves to have such experiences will obviously not attain their Godhood despite being part of the structure of the Divine. Overall, our dreams spell out that seeing proceeds from that which is there, and if that which is there is the Divine, we acquire the same character willy nilly. The term "that," as Martin Buber puts it, is "the eternal Presence of God or 'thou.'" God makes Himself known to us by exposing or showing us His manifest side. We have an eternal, divine companion in the form of the objective world. That which is there in front of us is not merely an object; it is the expression of the hidden side of the deity. It is the One but manifests itself in myriad forms. All that we see is the outer side of Him; no matter where we look. The above remarks are born out by the following received dreams:

- *Know that anything seen is God.*
- *All that you see there is me.*
- *The known God is all there.*
- *See: the whole environment represents I.*
- *There is a tableau vivant that clamors "I am your double you."*
- *All is your double you.*
- *That which is there is the stand of the Divine.*
- *There you see the external form of me.*
- *All that is there is the expression of the one.*
- *The Divine's total being is your companion.*
- *Always see that I am with you.*
- *My face is evident wherever you look.*
- *You cannot find a soul destitute of me.*

- My manifest side reflects itself in everyone without their permission.

Dreams that are more explicit on the topic of the divinity of humans due to the power of seeing are voluminous; below are a number of them:

- *That which you see there is me (God).*
- *See: God is there just before your eyes.*
- *What you see is me.*
- *Don't forget that the whole physical world represents my outer being.*
- *What you see there is my objective side.*
- *I am everything; there is nothing that is not me.*
- *What is evident is the manifest side of mine.*
- *The physical world is evidence of the oneness of my being.*
- *I am just what is visible.*
- *Your consciousness comprises my being.*
- *That which is there provides feed for your seeing (self).*
- *Attached to your seeing is the objective side of my being.*
- *My outer side is the owner of your self.*
- *What constitutes your self is my outer side.*
- *Self is seeing me.*
- *You see me as you turn your eyes in any direction.*
- *Self is the seeing of God.*
- *My outer side has lineaments that make your seeing possible.*
- *Always I am the content of your seeing (self).*
- *My outer side gives birth to you as a seeing being.*
- *You, as a conscious entity, have existence due to my presence.*
- *As you see, you attach a part of me to yourself.*
- *That which you see at every instant is my face.*
- *You are because I am.*
- *You perceive me even if I say I don't exist.*
- *You acquire genuine self when you recognize that which is beyond you is yourself.*

In a word, we possess a self or we become genuine humans only when we recognize ourselves as beings who are parts of God, a topic which will be discussed in the next chapter.

Summary

Acquiring identity with the Divine or union with the Deity is the doctrine of many mystics and the majority of the Eastern traditions; in addition, the principle of unity of all things has been accepted by many physicists. My dreams have consistently repeated that humans are not separate from the Divine. Those who have not experienced their union with the Divine and see themselves separate from Him have a make-believe identity; they have not learned about their true nature. We need to become aware that as self our real identity is one with that of the Divine. The difference between the revelations of our received dreams and the status of deification taught by other traditions is in the definition of man and God. Our received dreams make a distinction between humans who see themselves bound within the skin and humans who realize their genuine self which transcends the skin. Also the idea that most people have of God is that He is a concrete phenomenon in the heaven, not a verb or a form of inter-relation as described by Spinoza.

Our dreams substantiate the theme of the Deity of humans on three grounds. First, they state specifically and unequivocally that humans, whether they know it or not, are all parts of the Divine. When we see ourselves separate from Him, we are beside ourselves. We assume undue credit and pride for the things that all come to us spontaneously. Second, we are divine due to the all-inclusiveness of the Deity. If He is all, we are part of Him. A substantial number of my dreams specify that the Divine is all. Third, our divinity is based on the fact that we are seeing beings. We are created and owned by the objects we see or think about successively. Seeing or thinking come about when there is a seen or an object with which to occupy our thoughts. If the object we see or think about is the manifest side of the Divine, we become divinized due to the mere act of seeing although we may be totally unaware of this process. Furthermore, those who become aware of this process obtain divine identities or their true self as a result.

The point that our dreams seem to stress is this: if we see ourselves as gods or parts of Him, we give away the ordinary concept that we have of ourselves. We see all the world as parts of ourselves and take care of things as a wise God would. This is the topic that will be taken up again in the last chapter of this book. As a tree is not independent from the ground on which it has grown, we do not see ourselves independent from God's world, which at every juncture provides food for the body and content for our thoughts and consciousness. This is perhaps the reason why union with God is rightly called "salvation" in Christianity.

Chapter 8

The Relation of the Self to the Divine

The existence of parts implies a whole.

~Gustav Fechner

He who would save his life, will lose it.

~Luke 9:24

The whole can, under certain conditions, also become enfolded in all its parts. Thus each part represents the whole as in holograms.

~Karl Pribram

IN THE LAST three chapters, it was discussed that humans as self and the Divine are alike in several respects, that the Divine can best be defined as "I am that I am and that the self is one with the Divine. In this chapter, we explore the nature of the relation between humans as self and the Divine based on received dreams. The relation is somewhat more intricate than the previous discussions since its implication is this important question: If the self is part of the Divine, does this imply that by uniting with the Divine our own existence comes to an end or our identity remains intact by this union? As we shall see the answer depends again on how the self is defined or conceived.

The Doctrine of Self-Abandonment

Based on our dreams, the idea that almost everybody has of the self is false because it is inculcated by parents or people who have had no self-knowledge themselves. Thus, the concept or the notion we have of ourselves as independent, self-derived, or self-existent beings must be abandoned. It is an illusion, and we need to disillusion ourselves to find our genuine self or become real. The need for such disillusionment has been taught by many thinkers or mystics under such titles as self-abandonment, self-dissolution, self-renunciation, self-naughting, self-mortification, self-denial, self-surrender, selflessness, egolessness and so on. The goal of such teaching has been to eliminate the delusory notion people have of themselves that they are independent and separate from the Divine or from others.

Before dealing with the dreams, we will first quote thoughts or doctrines of some other well-known sources on the topic. In the Bible, we read: "He, who would save his life, will lose it" (Luke 9:24). The Egyptian-Roman philosopher Plotinus observed: "The final goal is the ecstasy in which all our finite personality and self-consciousness drops away, and we melt to a oneness with the Absolute wherein no shade of difference enters."[1] In the 9th century, John Scotus Erigena declared: "God is everything that truly is….This is the end of all things visible and invisible, when all visible things pass into intellectual, and the intellectual into God, by the marvelous and unspeakable union."[2]

In the Middle East, Persian philosopher Al-Hallaj, who was tortured and executed for saying *Anal-Hagh,* (I am the truth, or I am God) remarked: "I am He whom I love and He whom I love is I. We are two spirits dwelling in one body."[3] Again a Persian poet and a Sufi, Abu Said ibn Abi-I-Khir said:

> "He who sees you (referring to God) will lose himself. He who knows you knows not himself."

In France in the 12th century, monk and mystic Bernard of Clairveu noted: "To love yourself as if you no longer existed, to cease completely to experience yourself, to reduce yourself to nothing, is not a human sentiment but a divine experience…"[4]

Perhaps one of the most prominent exponents of the doctrine of human-divine identity is Meister Eckhart, who maintained creature or qua-creature does not exist. Whatever being creature possesses is not its own, it is God's property. He wrote: "God expects but one thing of you and that is you should come out of yourself in so far as you are a created being and let God be God in you."[5] Similarly, French philosopher Nicolas de Malebranche noted: "I derive nothing whatever from my own nature, nothing from the nature imagined by philosophers—all comes from God and His decrees."[6]

In the monotheistic religion of Sikhism, founded in the late 15th century, final salvation for humans is *Nirvana* or absorption into God's being like water blending with water. The Sikh looks on existence as a countless series of cycles until finally the separation is overcome, and the worshipper achieves complete union with God.[7] In the same vein, English Quaker leader William Penn, founder of Pennsylvania pointed out "We have nothing that we can call our own, no, not ourselves; for we are all but tenants of the great Lord of ourselves." Aldous Huxley explained the abandonment of the self to God in this way: "To the extent, there is an attachment to "I," "me," "mine," there is no attachment to the Divine ground."[8]

The following passage from Allan Watts' book *Supreme Identity* expresses well the attitude of those who truly abandon themselves.

> "He wills his total experience at this moment, and finds that it is not himself what wills, but God willing it in him. He surrenders himself without reserve to this moment's experience as the will of God and through surrender discovers perfect freedom.... Willingness to be insecure is the ultimate security. Willingness to suffer is the essence of divine joy. Willingness to be finite is to know one's own infinity. Willingness to be a slave is truly to be free. Willingness to be a fool and sinner is to be both a sage and a saint."[9]

Finally, a word from Carlos Castaneda: "Upon learning 'to see,' a man becomes everything by becoming nothing."

My dreams, in some respects, are in accord with the views expressed above. The received dreams repeatedly have hinted that the influence of the culturally imposed self that sees itself separate from the Divine and others must be neutralized, but our dreams do not say that the concept or memory that we have of ourselves or our past should be wiped out. As noted earlier, in a way, our sanity depends on our memories or past experiences. Our dreams show our union with the Divine is based on the nature of the self, which is spelled out as equivalent to consciousness, seeing, or a verb. As observed in several contexts before, the self as seeing comes about due to the existence of the physical, objective world, to which our dreams refer as the manifest side of the Divine.

At any moment, a piece of the outer, objective world forms the inner side of the self. Thus we become connected to the Divine spontaneously or automatically. If the contents of our seeing and thinking overcome us spontaneously, how can we claim being the owner of them? The more we think about the nature of the self, the more we find that all is originated from the outer world. We have nothing that can provide content for the self as consciousness or seeing. In addition, if the outer world is all the manifest side of the Divine, and if this side provides content for ourselves as seeing, then our union with the Divine becomes unquestionable. Therefore, when we forget ourselves, we become entities who are seeing Him and therefore being Him.

The following dreams indicate that the idea we have of ourselves is illusory:

- *The concept you have of your reality is unreal.*
- *When you reach here, your separateness ends.*
- *You should let go of the will-power or of the self which was the source of your problem.*
- *When you think of yourself being independent and separate, you have a wrong conception of yourself.*
- *That self that you thought you had was fake, you should let go of it.*
- *The concept that you have of yourself as a self-acting being must be given up.*

The following dreams reveal that we are not separate from the Divine:

- *If the Divine provides all that makes you tick, how can you be separate from him?*

- *If you see and think because of His world, are you not connected to Him?*
- *Remember that, which is there, gives rise to your self.*
- *You do not have any existence separate from the Divine's existence.*
- *If "that" which gives rise to your seeing (self) is outside your skin then "that" should be your identity.*
- *Your whole being is the Divine's being.*
- *As a conscious being, your reality is the product of that which is there (the manifest side of the Divine).*
- *My being lies in your seeing (your consciousness).*
- *If your identity arises from that which is there, how could you conceive yourself to be separate from it?*
- *In the scheme of things your separate "I" has no place.*
- *What do you have in your mental stock that you think you have originated it?*
- *You must set aside your old self to make room for the new integrated one.*
- *When consciousness is emptied of the make-believe self, it will be filled with the divineness.*

Based on our received dreams, if we have a self that believes it is separate from others or if it conceives that humans, as individuals, create all their abilities and potentials, such self-concepts are unreal. Our dreams point out such concepts of the self cause us a great deal of pain and problems. We might say with such self-concepts, life will be wasted in inane trivialities, paltry endeavors, and wanton pleasures. Material success becomes equivalent with happiness. We spend all our energy to compete with others, be better than others, or be as good as others. We strive to impress others by extreme superfluities and become preoccupied with such fancies as how good do I look, what kind of house, car, or gadget should I have? As a result, we frequently experience disappointment, rejection, or dejection.

We often feel anger, envy, fear, shame, or guilt due to the misconception we have of ourselves. Sometimes we blame ourselves mercilessly for events which really had nothing to do with us or which have been of no great matter. In short, when we have no knowledge of our real self, we devote our lives to banal, purposeless pursuits. We consistently and persistently play the role that our ignorant significant others unconsciously assigned to us, largely in childhood. At this point, the author of this book needs to acknowledge he, despite being a psychologist, does not absolve himself from undergoing experiences similar to those mentioned above, if not currently, but at least for a good portion of his life. What our dreams teach us is that the unreal self-concept must be neutralized so that such misery comes to an end, and there can be room for the growth of a new being.

Self as Part of the Whole

In the previous section, the teachings of our dreams were that the ego or separate-self must be abandoned or its influence be curbed. Our dreams have specified that since God is all-inclusive, we must let go of the concept of separateness. On the other side, if there be no individual with distinct self-awareness, the concept of God or the whole universe remains unknown. As some mystics have remarked: "If I as a lover vanish, my beloved will have no one to love her." Thus, the question arises: If God and man are one, or if we let the individual merge with God, what happens to God? A Hindu devotional classic puts the matter thus: "I want to taste the sugar; I don't want to be sugar."

This section will explore the status of the self when the ego is superseded. The main message of our dreams is that self based on the principle "I am that I am" becomes a multitude or becomes all that it sees, and since all that it sees, at any moment, is God, self becomes "parts" and parcel of God.

Thus, the relation between humans, possessing selves, and God is viewed in terms of category of parts and whole. The relation can be characterized as a kind of union in which the identity of the individual is not lost. We do not vanish. We still exist but as parts of the Divine, not separate from Him as was the case when the ego was dominant. Past life experiences that have led to the formation of ego are not obliterated but are rendered innocuous. As a new being, we do not see ourselves as self-sufficient and wholly independent entities. We gain the awareness that we are parts of the whole and driven by the wisdom and the energy of the whole or God.

Based on the dicta of our received dreams, when we fully comprehend that we are connected to the Divine then we come to the possession of our true selves and to the realization that we are nothing more than a segment of the whole being. Many thinkers have supported this viewpoint. Parmenides believed that the individual is incapable of assuming an independent status apart from All. Marcus Aurelius held that we are parts of the Deity who acts in us.[10] Every man alike forms a part of the being of God. The Bible tells us: "In God, we live and move and have our being" (Acts 17:28). When both Jewish and Christian scholars were discussing God's knowledge of his creature, they could not accept that the creatures were external objects to God, about whom God could know the contingent truth. In this connection, Spinoza declared: "We must remember that our mind is so far as it truly perceives things a part of the infinite intellect of God."[11] Josiah Royce observed: "The absolute experience is related to human experience as an organic whole to its integral fragments."[12]

As we saw in chapter 6, God is the name of the whole visible and invisible dimensions of being of whom all finite beings are mere parts. Humans and everything in nature are constituents of His being. As Hegel puts it (when we speak of) "the total world order, embracing the inorganic, the organic, and the spiritual level of existence is one all-inclusive order, we speak of the Absolute or God." Humans are all like fragments of him.[13] A number of our dreams specify that the Divine is the whole and we are the parts of Him. The examples of such dreams are:

- *The total being of the Divine is expressed in the internal and the external worlds.*
- *The Divine is the whole; hence He consists of everyone and everything.*
- *You are part of us.*
- *You are parts and parcel of the whole.*
- *Know the Divine is the whole.*
- *I (God) represent the whole.*
- *Thou art in me.*
- *You need to give yourself (the make-believe self) away.*

Perhaps again the relation of the self to the Divine can best be presented graphically, based on my interpretations of the dreams I have received. In chapter 3, we used Figure 1 to show the dynamic character of the self. In chapter 6, we used Figure 2 to show the dynamic character of the Divine. All we have to do now is to superimpose Figure 1 over Figure 2 to show how we as parts fit into the whole divine configuration at any instant.

Humans as Parts; Divine as Whole

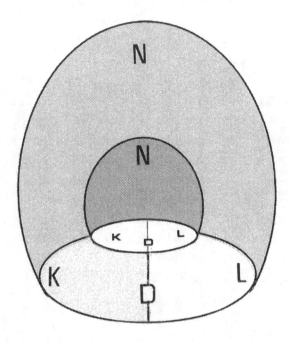

Figure 3: The Divine and the self structures are similar in that both have a subjective (N) and an objective side (D) Also the objective side of both have a two-fold character.

The objective side of the self consists of the organism and the environment and that of the Divine presumably consists of time and space although we are not certain about the last two named terms since our dreams have not specifically labeled them. Figure 3 represents one instant or one point in an infinitesimal space of time, disregarding all past instants or periods.

We have had many dreams that confirm the configuration represented by Figure 3. Here is a sample of them:

- *You are both in my subjective and objective side.*
- *What is there is both you and the Divine.*
- *You have two IDs, one comes from this side of mine, the other from that side of mine.*
- *You share your physical side with my physical side and your non-physical with my non-physical.*
- *You and I are both manifest there.*
- *The particulars of yours and mine are both shown there.*
- *That which appears there at any instant is my being as well as your being.*
- *You have to create your own face through the use of my face.*
- *Like you, I am plurality as object, unity as subject.*
- *Remember the principle "I am that I am" applies both to you and me.*
- *I am in you and you are in me.*
- *Your outer half has a twofold character; so has mine.*
- *K and L stand for your outer side as well as mine.*

Self as a Part which is the Whole

Based on the dreams quoted in the preceding section, we are evidently parts of the Divine. The question that remains to be answered is this: Are we mere parts or are we a part that is a minute copy of all? The dreams that will be presently included indicated that we are a part that is in some sense a whole too. The fact that no element of this universe is really separate from the whole presupposes a kind of overall cohesiveness that makes a part also the whole. Another point that needs to be repeatedly recalled is that our received dreams are not dealing with the physical side of our lives; rather, they deal with the inner nature of humans which represents consciousness or seeing in its special sense, and consciousness or seeing, according to our dreams imply boundlessness and extra-finiteness.

Again the topic of the part being equal to the whole has been subject of deliberation of many thinkers in various periods of history. To name a few, we include the following: Buddha advised us, "Once we attain self-realization, we see clearly that we are all, we know all for we are all." Parmenides said, "The only true being is the one and the one cannot be divided because the whole of it is present everywhere."[14] Plotinus held;

"Each being contains in self, the whole, intelligible world. Therefore all is everywhere. Each is there All, and all is each."[15] Leibniz's position was that God was a monad. "In a monadic organization, the parts contain the whole as in the hologram."[16] In other words, each part represents or contains the whole as each individual part of the picture contains the whole picture in a hologram.

Similarly, Bruno, the Italian philosopher and astronomer, who was burned at the stake by the Inquisition, maintained God is the whole, but a whole that is present in its completeness in each single part. Thus "man is all of God….Each man is a point in which the fullness of God reflects. God is present in the blade of grass, in the grain of sand, in the atoms that float, in the sunbeam as well as in the boundless All."[17] Bruno, without being aware, repeated what apparently was said by Buddha long before him: "All in each and each in all."[18]

Dreams that we had confirming the self as parts equal to the whole are many and varied. Here are some specimens:

- *In every particle there is the property of all other particles.*
- *Any being contains all.*
- *Your inner side contains the whole world.*
- *You carry all of the divine being.*
- *The object of your subjective side is all of the Divine. (Hence the subjective side becomes all of the Divine too.)*
- *A God who is all begets a God who is all.*
- *Inside of you is all of the Divine.*
- *All is being you.*
- *You too own all of the Divine's external world.*
- *You don't find a part in which does not subsist all of the whole.*
- *Everything is the miniature of one.*
- *As one over nine (1/9) results in infinite ones, so anything as one over nine is infinite.*
- *The Divine being is attached to you.*
- *You are all of the Divine's being.*

The previous statements enunciated in our dreams appear to the author as incredible as perhaps it does to some readers, but all that can be said in this connection is that the author has faithfully reflected what his dreams have dictated.

Some have questioned if God is the whole, does that not leave the human self as a mere name? Presumably, the answer, according to our received dreams, is: humans, as parts of the Divine, are a kind of being, who can understand that the object they see is part of themselves. Without the object, they can have no seeing, no consciousness, no mind, and if the physical world that humans see is also the manifest side of the Divine, man becomes divine simply due to the mere process of seeing. The object produces the seeing of the subject. If the object is the Divine, the human as subject becomes thus Divinized.

Therefore the human self shares the outer world with the Divine in a degree that it sees, understands, and thus incorporates the outer world. In this manner, humans as parts of the Divine are challenged to explore and discover the nature of things in the physical world. One might surmise if the human self could explore and understand everything in the world, we could become as great as God himself, but since this is inconceivable, we, as finite beings, always remain parts of His infinite being. Therefore, to possess a deified status is more than a mere name. Being endowed with the gift of rationality, with the power of seeing, as self and as parts, we can even claim that we have the potential to become the discoverer and revealer of the Divine in His entirety.

Summary

A most vital question facing all is whether the self we think we have is fictitious and needs to be abandoned, or is it genuine and needs to be prized and elevated. Another fundamental question is, if we believe in God, how do we stand in relation to Him? In this chapter, in the context of our dreams, we attempted to find an answer to these questions. The conclusion, we have drawn from countless dreams is that the usual image we have of ourselves as beings separate from the Divine is erroneous; hence, such images must be replaced by a self-concept that experience itself is a part of the Divine. Samples of dreams confirming this conclusion were given.

According to our received dreams, we find a genuine self when we realize that we are all fragments of the Divine being; therefore, our task is to transcend the illusion of being separate from Him. If we succeed in this endeavor, the union of the self and the Divine will become a reality. The previous conceptions we have had of ourselves will not disappear; they will be integrated into our new conception of the self, hence will be divinized. We come to believe that we are parts of the Divine mainly because we are certain that the Divine represents the unifying whole and as such He embraces everything, humans in particular. We become convinced that what we see is the manifest side of the Divine and we, as seeing beings, become parts of Him as we see any object. By coalescing into Him we surrender a self that is unreal and realize a self that is real. Obviously we do not give up our past experiences. We only renounce a bunch of misconceptions we have had of ourselves that have kept us rootless, disorientated, and lost, causing us a great deal of problems and pain. Our new being, our divinized, well-integrated self will acquire a disposition or character which is not only free from negative emotions and conflicts but also is combined with harmony, serenity, deep peace and a feeling of at-homeness with the universe at large.

Chapter 9

Self as the Divine's Viceregent

The purpose of life is to become God and act as God.

~John Scotus

The goal of life is to see things truly as they exist for God.
Such a condition is the only true freedom.

~Gottfried Leibniz

Self is the goal of knowledge. Know self and go beyond death.

~The Upanishads

IN THIS CHAPTER, we propose to examine the role we have to play in life, according to our dreams. The conclusion reached is that we must participate in divinity. The end of the road is to learn what is meant by the self and God and how we, as selves, have to conduct our lives in relation to Him. In the preceding chapter, it was concluded that we are parts of the Divine. In this chapter, we want to explore the nature of our vocation or calling as parts of the Divine; or even better, what is the purpose of life in general?

The term that seems to fit our assignment in life is viceregent. Ibn al'Arabi observed: "God has created man in His own image to make him His viceregent."[1] Jewish tradition says God made man because He needed a partner in creation. He has chosen Israel to be his servant to bring man to a true knowledge of God. In Islam, there is a tradition, specifying that God has revealed to an earlier prophet this message: "I was a hidden treasure.

107

I desired to be known so I created the universe (human beings)."[2] This is apparently in line with Abraham's reply to the Lord when the Lord told him: "You would not exist if it were not for me." Abraham's reply was: "But, my Lord, you would not be known if it were not for me."[3] Hegel pointed out the role of humans in this connection more explicitly. "It is a fact that through human rationality that the Absolute has its being."[4] However, based on our received dreams, we have to do much more than making the Divine known.

It is vitally important to know what role the human has to play in the universe. Our dreams indicate that humans are created to act on behalf of the reign of God. It is self-evident that God has no hands to do material things around the world; He needs executors, who can carry out His plan. Thus humans, as parts of Him, are in a sense complementary to the Divine. The Persian poet Hafiz pointed this out in these words:

> "Heaven could not carry the burden (of implementing His plan). The lot fell upon man to make up for Heaven's handicap."

Consequently, God needs humans to become partners in creation, or one might say, He expects us all to act as his viceregents. Once we understand this we become infused with new vigor, new life, new courage, and new awareness of our vocation as human beings. We recognize that we are participants in God's creation. Our end becomes union with God and fulfilling our life task as workers worthy to have a place, so to speak, on the Divine team.

Dreams confirming the above viewpoints are:

- *Humans should do everything in my name.*
- *Humans should make manifest things that are unmanifest.*
- *I (the Divine) and the world will be known through the intellect of humans.*

Distinguishing Characteristics of Viceregents

As a viceregent, our central goal would be to live according to precepts that we believe are approvable by the Divine. We are aware that two types of self are operating in us: one that was imposed on us by parents and culture, telling us "You are such and such," "you should do or should not do this and that." We became unknowingly all their injunctions. As a consequence, we came to believe we are who they said we are. We became convinced that we are individuals, separate from others and should generally compete with others. The other type of self, which is the genuine self, is realizable when we become aware that what others told us about who we are was mostly untrue. It is then that we find a powerful urge to discover our real identity.

Ultimately, self-realization is self-realization in God. We come to find our true identity when we realize that we are really nothing separate from Him, but are everything when we see ourselves connected to Him. As Thomas Merton says: "We see that we ourselves are Adam, we ourselves are Christ, and we are dwelling in one another by virtue of the divine image…." Our real identity will be revealed to us, for the most part, through communion with the Divine in our dreams and through self-searching and self-contemplation. When the unreal belief systems are shaken up, the road will be paved for finding the new identity or new perception of reality. We see things in a totally different light. The new perception shows its influence in every part of our conduct. It is like adding water to a dying plant, it penetrates every segment of it; therefore, we will be able to affirm the will of the Divine as though an inner force spontaneously makes us do so. We feel united with Him and cooperate with Him in improving things in the world.

We realize that our beings can become real by transcending our factitious, old self and bringing ourselves into harmony with the reality of our divine nature. We discover our existential problems. We realize our place in the world is for some particular purpose. We experience a need for moving toward some goal. Overall, we become aware that we must be true partners of the Divine by reflecting his justice, compassion, and wisdom wherever and whenever we can. We devote ourselves to love all manifestations of life that call for such devotion.

The fact that we become convinced that we are Divine viceregents on earth leads us to adopt a new outlook on life, in at least four arenas. First, we reintegrate ourselves with the Divine consciously. We know that we have been misled by those who told us we are entities independent of others and God. Now we realize all that we possess comes from the Divine.

As such, we see ourselves as parts and parcel of the Divine. We have no doubt that our inner sides of life are united with Him. Hence, the Divine becomes the focal point of our thoughts, interests, and feelings. Spinoza said: "The good consists in mystical union with God."[5] Our dreams tell us that we are already parts of Him; the task is to recognize our role.

Second, as a viceregent we see God in everything. It was mentioned in chapter 6 that God, like humans, has an inner, invisible side and an outer, visible side. Based on our dreams all that we see with our own eyes is the visible side of the Divine. As a result, when we look out and see various kinds of objects, we see all of them as the outer manifestation of the Divine, even when we know they are human-made. Humans, as parts, could not have produced the objects, had the Divine not been active in them. We realize that nothing exists by itself and that everything depends on the Divine as one unifying entity. Thus we see everything as derivative of the Divine and sharing His nature. In particular, when in the presence of a person, first we regard him as a manifestation of God, then as the person known to us otherwise. This implies that we see everyone as parts of God and treat them with the same reverence that we show toward God. This kind of viewing people will keep us tranquil in nearly all interactions. A person who may hurt us with his remarks or his actions if visualized as part of ourselves or the Divine in action should immediately calm us due to our united experience.

Third, as a viceregent, we become more receptive to our dreams and consider them to be important messages from the Divine, aimed at helping us to become whole. As indicated in chapter 1, the messages for good reason are in code. Once we become interested in our dreams, gradually we learn the method of decoding them. We find a great mind in the universe, communicating with us in order to give us a more in-depth and meaningful life. The experience of the author of this work, outlined in chapter 1, may be of value to those who seek to follow this route and to hold communion with the Divine about things that really matter. It is presumed by such an approach, we may discover our true identity, or what Royce calls "the larger self," which consists both of that which is within and that which is without.

Fourth, as a viceregent, we engage in some form of self-monitoring or self-examination. We control the content of our mind. We do not allow daydreaming and fantasy about meaningless things to enter it. We recognize that in a way the worth and true measure of our lives depend on the content of our thoughts at any given moment. Do we think about matters emanating from our unreal self or our real self? Do we identify with our divine nature at times when we need to make a decision? Do we really see others when contacting them as the contents, as well as the creators of our mental life at that instant? Do we recognize that what we see at every moment is really our outer self as well as that of the Divine? We also engage in some sort of self-suggestion, preferably every morning, stressing upon our own minds that in this day I will act more in accord with my divine identity and less under the influence of the identity imposed on me.

Some received dreams directly or indirectly touch upon the characteristics of the viceregent are given below:

- *You should know that if you live with me, I will live with you too.*
- *You do not exist as an independent separate being.*
- *Human task is to make the Divine known and to divinize themselves.*
- *To attain divine consciousness, you have to look at objects as though you see the Divine.*
- *You must decide whether you want the old self to be in charge of your life or your divine self.*
- *To make room for your new self, you must do away with the old self.*
- *As you look at an object make sure that you see it as the manifest side of the Divine.*
- *Remember that which is in you and makes you go is the Divine himself.*
- *Check and see who is the company of your genuine self at any instant.*
- *Check and see if you are making God of all that you see.*
- *Bear in mind that there is a physical world so that the Divine can be seen constantly.*
- *Suggest to yourself that during this particular day "I will act as a part of the Divine."*
- *See if you experience the fact that others, without being aware, are giving rise to your inner self.*

- *Note if the objects that you behold have the lineament characteristics of the Divine rather than their mundane form.*
- *Remember that which you see there is God as well as you.*
- *Check to see that you are really acquiring a self out of everything you observe, and that everything you observe is Divine.*

The Viceregent as Divine Operator

In the previous section, the characteristics of the self as a viceregent were outlined; the emphasis was on the viceregent himself. In this section, we are concerned with the viceregent's relation in regard to others. Essentially, as executors, we have to meet two sets of basic needs of others; those of their physiological natures and those of their non-physiological natures. Our concerns for the needs of others are in a real sense a kind of enlightened self-interest since it is others who constitute our non-physiological nature or our genuine self. We fully recognize our dependence upon others because if there are no others, we will have no thoughts, no mind or, in truth, no self. Others are more vital for our total existence than our usual bodies. Readers, who have followed our discussion of the principle "I am that I am" should have no difficulty agreeing with what was just stated. It seems noteworthy to point out that Plato also held the world that lay beyond the sense as a justification of human effort.

As a viceregent, our duties toward others depend on a number of factors, including time, place, political, social, economic condition, components of culture and our own state of development and abilities. Whatever we propose to accomplish, we take into account its feasibility aspect first. There is no point in attempting things that are not capable of being done, executed, utilized, or affected. Thus anything we undertake to do must be within our powers. We should not forget the limits that all of us as humans have, despite the fact that in a special sense we are Divine.

The goal in all situations is the welfare and development of as many as we can reach. However, it is in the transpersonal realm that our proper task begins. The demand is made upon us is to participate in the new creation and to push the boundary of reality. We need to discover anew the genuine value of life and to share it with others. By bringing others to a true knowledge of God, by attending to a worthy cause, or by giving ourselves with loyalty and enthusiasm to something beyond ourselves, we find new meaning in life and fulfill our mission as viceregents faithfully. Examples of our dreams that refer to the task of viceregents are the following:

- *Humans need to attend as God to that which needs attention.*
- *One of the vocations of humans is to make the Divine known.*
- *The Divine has expressed itself in different locations with different forms. It is up to humans to discover their meaning.*
- *Human task is to explore the unexplored*
- *Put into practice whatever you learned from the dream messages.*
- *As my deputies, humans have infinite possibilities for service.*
- *Your inner world will find meaningful content as you engage in things that need caring and devotion.*
- *Acknowledge to your self that you are the executor of the Divine's plans.*
- *Do only that which can be done.*

Standard of Conduct

As viceregents, when we want to choose carefully a course of action or a method of performing our tasks, what standard or guidelines do we have for our purpose? Spinoza teaches us that we act according to God's decree and are participants in the divine nature. John Scotus says: "The purpose of life is to become God and act as God, and those who have achieved this stage are to show their way to others."[6] Leibniz also holds: "The goal of life is to see things truly as they exist for God. Such a condition is the only true freedom."[7] Martin Buber's view is that "the relation with man is the real simile of the relation with God."[8] According to our dreams, we must acquire a God's eye view in whatever we do. All we have to do is what is it that He wants us to do in this situation. In a spirit of being his proxy, we undertake our day-to-day tasks. Thus we pursue life activities in the way we believe He thinks it should be done. We should remember that we humans have all been endowed with intelligence, understanding, and power of reasoning in order to use all of these for creating greater good. This is particularly true when we see ourselves as viceregents and as parts of the Divine. In such a role, we regard our own nature and norms to be in accord with the Divine's nature.

Some of our received dreams that are specific about criteria to be followed with regard to the performance of our calling as viceregents are:

- *You imagine yourself in the Divine's shoes.*
- *Do it in the way you believe He thinks it should be done.*
- *Regard things as they are as the Divine plan as well as a challenge. Improve them as far as possible.*
- *What is there is a kind of guide and guru.*
- *Consider what you see to be there as a non-verbal Bible.*
- *"That" which is there is the way.*
- *That which is there is the will of the Divine.*
- *In every situation, act as though the Divine is present.*
- *In every case, let reason prevail, bearing in mind that the Divine is the source of rationality.*
- *The standard with which you can decide good and bad is whether a thing is good or bad for a fruitful life.*
- *You will hear from the Divine as you identify more and more with Him.*
- *Often you will receive feedback as to how appropriate your action has been.*
- *Forget what you like, make sure that the Divine will approve of what you are doing.*
- *Whatever has been created is good; if it was bad it would not have been created.*

Blessings of a Viceregent

The reward for feeling parts of the Divine or for realizing the divinized self is immense. By subduing the imperative of the old, unreal self, by vanquishing senseless thoughts, and by curbing all unnecessary expectations and desires, we really feel free. In particular, when we stop living up to the expectations of those who are trammeled by their unreal selves, we become greatly liberated. No longer do we have anything to lose, nor have we any need for affectation or self-justification. We overcome all kinds of fears as we become convinced that we are parts of a wise larger whole. As Marcus Aurelius said: "We expect nothing, we fear nothing," or as the Upanishads says:

"He who knows the self is unaffected whether by good or evil. Neither do such thoughts come to him: I have done an evil thing or I have done a good thing. Both good and evil, he has transcended and he is therefore troubled no more."

When the self is imbued with the Divine character, we will be transported with joy. We celebrate the fact that we are parts of the Divine, and we have sense organs capable of seeing variety, multiplicity, craftsmanship and artistry everywhere. It seems as though the Divine has furnished His outer side, His physical world, with a museum containing sceneries and creatures with splendid designs, perfect systems and coloration. After realizing our deified self when we observe these wondrous exquisite creations; we first become elated that we are able to see the splendor of the manifest side of the Divine, then based on the principle "I am that which I see," it dawns on us again and again that those wonders that surround us are not only the Divine but the outer half of ourselves too. Such experiences bring us tremendous fascination and delight. A feeling of intense bliss overcomes us when we come to realize that the beautiful things we see all over reflect our own self in truth.

As viceregents, we always remember this basic fact that the real self consists of "seeing" in its special sense and the essence of seeing is its content. This knowledge provides us with power to change the state of our own beings almost instantly. If the essence of our beings is seeing then all it takes to transform our unpleasant or painful mood is to shift our seeing, our attention, to that which is pleasant and soothing. Instead of dwelling on the painful condition that supplies content for our self or our seeing, we look at those parts of creations which can bring peace and serenity. This method of thought control and attention redirection has been practiced by professional and non-professional in all ages. The difference between what was mentioned above and what has been practiced by others is the degree of appreciation. In our deified state, we appreciate the positive things of life to an extent that is not generally possible by those who are in their old selves. Moreover, those with deified selves have greater endurance for adversity and calamity due their conviction that whatever happens is ultimately right.

Another blessing of being a viceregent is that human life will find meaning and purpose. The way most of us conduct our lives currently is pointless or senseless. We go to school, find a job, work hard, obtain and consume a certain amount of food, acquire a number of household items and save some money. We also socialize, meet friends and relatives. We watch T.V., games or sports events, spend time with our computer, phone, IPhone, IPad, or with Twitter, Instagrams, Youtube, etc. In most situations, we had to undergo immense struggle and stress in order to find a job, to maintain it, and to please various bosses.

None of those events named above are bad; in fact, considering the demand of the reality confronting us, all of these activities may be necessary. However, the main question still remains: Is this all life is about; are we here to lead life in such a manner and then disappear? It was suggested earlier that our rationality is the Divine's rationality. Using this gift and viewing the state of affairs of the world within our purview, Can we really say we are here to follow such patterns of existence?

Our received dreams as well as our reasoning powers indicate that the purpose of life is what a benevolent God would want to do Himself if He were on earth, taking into account the limitations imposed on us by time, place, circumstances, and our own capabilities. We feel fulfilled and indeed serve the purpose of life just by keeping such a goal or calling in mind and by doing all that is possible by us.

Some dreams that refer to the positive things that will attend the life of viceregents are given below:

- *Any kind of fear indicates lack of faith.*
- *Once you become enlightened, you do not demand very much; when ignorant, you never get satisfied with what you have.*
- *As part of God, you become needless.*
- *If you really see the Divine as your permanent company, you will never feel lonely.*
- *If the Divine is your owner, He will take good care of you.*
- *You will have peace of mind when you become united with the Divine.*
- *If you can see the Divine in charge, you will be free.*
- *When you can see things as the Divine sees them, you experience life differently.*

- *It is up to the father (the Divine) where He wants to take the child (human). As a human being, it is important to know where the child goes, but it is more important to know that the father will take care of him properly.*

Life After Death

Perhaps the greatest of all blessings is the attainment of eternal life. Many traditions and religions believe in the doctrine of life after death or immortality although most of them discard the notion of personal immortality or physical resurrection. The Jews believe in immortality and the resurrection of the spirit. Christians and Moslems more or less equally believe in reward and punishment in the hereafter. Many philosophers also believed in life after death. The famous Pythagoras, who considered himself to be a semi-divine being, taught that the soul is immortal; it is something that gets transformed into a different form of living. Also Socrates, Plato, and Plotinus all believed in immortality. Plato's argument was if ideas are immortal, the soul must be immortal too. Aristotle's view in this connection was not very clear. He said the soul is not immortal, but intellect (nous) is. The later Stoics also held that the soul is immortal.

To Thomas Aquinas, the immortality of the soul can be proven by natural reason. Spinoza expresses his view on life after death thus: "Man arrives in God, lives in God and it is in the very concrete sense that he himself is divine. Through propinquity to God, one becomes eternal." Spinoza rejects the personal immortality adhered to by Christianity but holds that the impersonal soul that consists in becoming more and more one with God will become eternal.

Descartes also thought the survival in a disembodied state after death of the body is at least logically possible. The position of Kant and William James on immortality is very much alike. Both justify immortality on the grounds of faith, moral values, and the deep craving of humans. German philosopher, founder of phenomenology, Edmund Husserl, seems to say what our dreams reveal on this topic. Some have criticized him saying that he holds some rather extreme views on transcendental ego as he said more than once that:

"This ego (a synonym for the term "self"as used by our dreams)

117

would remain in existence even if the entire world were destroyed and that this ego is an individual entity distinct from the self which is the object of my empirical self-observation. It sounds as if I had two selves, one of them, the familiar empirical one, and the other transcendental and generally unknown one which would remain in existence even if my empirical self were destroyed with the destruction of the world."[9]

Idris Shah quotes an allegory used by the Sufis to illustrate the transmutation that takes place in human existence through mortality.[10] The gist of the allegory runs as follows…

"A stream ran for a while but reached a desert and found it could not proceed anymore. The water was disappearing into the fine sand constantly. The stream became desperate and began complaining. A voice said: 'Allow yourself to be carried by the wind so that when the wind drops the moisturized sand in another land a new stream can flow. There you will find that you are the same stream that you are today. You may be called by a different name but the essence of you will know that you are the same stream. Today you know yourself only by the attributes others ascribed to you. Really you do not know which part of you is your true essence.' At this point the stream acknowledged: 'Now I am beginning to understand something about my true identity.'"

Our dreams seem to uphold the state of immortality. Based on the principle "I am that which I see." If that, as discussed earlier, is the manifest side of the Divine, we become divinized with every instance of seeing, provided the object seen is acknowledged being the Divine. Obviously, when we view things in this manner, the memory we form is a divinized memory. Considering Figure 3, all the memories we form will also become parts of the memory of the Divine. Therefore, by virtue of the fact that He is eternal, we become eternal also. Moreover, we learn from the principles of physics that the total energy involved in a process is always conserved. The self is a form of energy and energy never vanishes, or as Josiah Royce says: "Nothing that has been shall ever be lost or forgotten." One way to understand how life after death is possible is to look at our own dreams. In them all kinds of phenomena become active without requiring any space. The above remarks reflected the views of some well-known thinkers. The actual dream messages bearing on the topic of immortality are cited below:

- *The self is eternal.*
- *A consciousness comprised of seeing objects as Divine will become immortal.*
- *Death and dying are characteristics of the temporal world.*
- *People who had the experience of divinity will remain; they will not be perished.*
- *The Divine preserves those who become parts of Him.*
- *The deified persons never die.*
- *You have to become more convinced about the future life.*
- *All that you have experienced as Divine becomes parts of your future life.*
- *Life resumes a different form but essentially it is your self.*
- *The life of those who became one with the Divine is eternal.*
- *The inner half of the self is immortal.*
- *You, as memory, will remain.*
- *The past does not disappear.*
- *To become one with the Divine and to be mortal at the same time is impossible.*

Summary

Through the insistent and consistent messages of the received dreams, we realize that not only are we parts of the Divine, but we are also His deputies or viceregents on earth. We see, what Plato said, that the world which lies beyond the senses is justification for our efforts. The Divine has bestowed a self or a mind with which to know Him and to identify with Him. Once we are aware that we are parts of Him, and we are here for a purpose, we also come to the realization that we must make the Divine known. Without the intelligence of humans, the Divine would remain unknown, and to make Him known, all we have to do is to recognize and teach that whatever exists represents the external side of the Divine. As we identify with the Divine, we transcend our old self-concept and acquire a new conception of ourselves and the Divine. We realize that the self arises from others and includes others. Associated with this conception is a feeling of unity or oneness with all things, a feeling of sharing, a common fate or a striving for a common goal. In reality, this means a new birth into life. Hence, our great and noble calling becomes to discover anew the genuine worth of human life and to share it with others. On the whole, we rely on our own resources but become a lamp into ourselves.

Our task or mission is essentially practical and worldly. We act in accordance, with our real nature. As viceregents, we feel a definite responsibility for serving the benefit of mankind and the relief of society. We become as benevolent as God himself. We give freely of ourselves. We give up our selfish goals. Out of the many forms of service, the ones we choose will be those which are timely and worthwhile. Our God-given lives will be spent in pursuit of projects that yield the greatest possible benefit. The standard we employ in dealing with others is commensurate with our rank as viceregents. We see the Divine having a real presence in every transaction. We consider others, who, at the time of transaction, are, in effect, the creator of our inner world, as better parts of ourselves. The thought of taking advantage of them never crosses our minds.

Blessings that are conducive to our happiness and intensified sense of well-being are numerous. We live spontaneously in accord with the Divine or natural laws. Knowing that Divine power is working in us, we achieve a heightened sense of reality, feeling at home in the universe at large. We experience a kind of signification, beauty, and awe, which is hard to put into words. Our way of living becomes simple and undemanding. There will no longer be any desire for competition, ambition, or for becoming better or greater than others since we know others are really ourselves. All such false inclinations fall away. The consequence of such a life is peace of mind, deep satisfaction, and bliss. Moreover, external happening will not impact us considerably. We will be calmer, more active, and freer. Above all, we become convinced that our lives do not really end. There is a form of life better and different from the one we had on earth that is awaiting us. In short, if we realize a self that is part of the Divine and act as a divine agent on earth, the life after death becomes a reality for us, based on our received dreams.

Epilogue

THE NUMEROUS SHORT dreams quoted in the body of this book were largely translated, decoded, or, in a few cases, extrapolated to tell the intended meaning in more comprehensible terms. To better enable the curious readers to judge for themselves the veracity of our presentation, we quote in this section, a small sample of dreams received, all in English, bearing on the topics discussed. The dreams included in this section are all verbatim. They present the concepts discussed in rather plain, understandable English. As such, they at least serve two purposes. First, they round out adequately the ideas presented in this book. Second, they allow the reader perhaps to come up with meanings different from what has been inferred by this author. As far as this author can discern, the dreams to be quoted correspond fully with the dreams largely translated for each chapter of the book.

From the discussion of the topic of dreams in chapter 1, we concluded that in dreams, God speaks to us, for good reasons almost always in code to enable us to understand who we are, who He is, and how we should conduct our lives. The following dreams attest to what was just stated.

- *Dreams are God's words.*
- *Through dreams I talk to humans to awaken them.*
- *Everything in dreams is symbolic.*
- *Dreams represent my speaking part.*
- *Dreams are the important aspect of reality.*
- *There is a lot of stuff that only dreams can produce.*
- *Dreams talk about three areas (human, Divine, and their relationship).*

Chapter 2 considers the messages of the dreams pertaining to human identity. They make it clear that our true nature consists of all that we see beyond us at any moment. In the following dreams, this viewpoint is expressed unambiguously:

- *The first thing that needs to receive attention is the self.*
- *To know self is know reality.*
- *What you think is yourself is not yourself.*
- *All you are proceeds from the physical world. You must receive impact from the non-physical world to become your true self.*
- *Consciousness is reality.*
- *Consciousness is equivalent to seeing.*
- *Your being is comprised of consciousness.*
- *You, as self, dwell in your seeing.*
- *What you see there is your real identity.*
- *The environment is your root.*
- *You must be there to be born (moment by moment).*
- *When you see yourself to be there you will find a place here.*
- *You see your own picture in everything you look at.*
- *You are sitting there.*
- *Thou art that. (that is the content of thy thought)*
- *The subject is obtained with the presence of an object.*
- *The self belongs to that.*
- *The self and reality are one.*

In chapter 3, the ramification of the self as "I am that" is elaborated by presenting a model (Figure 1). The received dreams specify that the self has two sides: a side which is manifest but in itself is without consciousness or life and a side which is unmanifest but possesses consciousness or life. As the two sides interact, each side realizes itself in the unity of motion or activity inherent in the verb "seeing." The following dreams refer to this configuration.

- *So we have two halves.*
- *There is an invisible side to every visible side.*
- *The visible keeps the invisible alive.*
- *The outer begets the inner.*

- *The visible is the manifestation of the invisible.*
- *Your inner side, like a particle, floats in the air.*
- *You are situated in the space from which you can see your doings. Others do not see you. They see your objective side.*
- *That side which sees is not a thing.*
- *The organism and environment form the objective side of your seeing.*
- *You go in cycle.*
- *The outer world is the objective self.*

Transcendency of the self is treated in chapter 4. Based on the received dreams, the concept of the self, as seeing, actualizes as it goes beyond itself, appropriating an object or experiencing the past or conceiving its unity. Dreams confirming the transcendency of the self include:

- *The self is transcendental.*
- *The outer world is the objective self.*
- *As we get outside ourselves, we can look at ourselves.*
- *Without traveling, seeing becomes impossible.*
- *There are whole areas of you which are beyond you (beyond your body).*
- *In essence, you are the real world.*
- *You end at that end (you extend as far as you see).*
- *If everything is an experience, your self carries them because of all the experiences it has had, there (the outer world) is the limit of you.*

The doctrine that the Divine and humans are connatural or consubstantial is dealt with in chapter 5. It is indicated that the self of the human shares the nature of the Divine in at least seven areas: both denote being, both are of the nature of activity, both have the power of seeing, both are dipolar, having a non-physical and a physical side, both express unity and both exhibit a great deal of intelligence. Dreams that speak to this connaturality are as follows:

- *Everything is God.*
- *The evidence for the existence of God is overwhelming.*
- *God and human nature are the same.*

- *Characteristics of both (self and God) are one.*
- *Man (self) and God are alike.*
- *I am like you.*
- *I am consciousness so you are.*
- *We are nothing other than seeing (other than consciousness).*
- *Seeing is all.*
- *Whatever is, is seeing.*
- *The outer world shows the identity of both the Divine and the human.*
- *He has shared his identity with humans.*

What was set forth in chapter 6 seems to be in line with the self-identification of God in the Old Testament (Exodus 3:13-14) when God said unto Moses: "I am that I am." If we accept the definition of "I am that which I see" for the self of humans, it should not be difficult to accept the same ascription for the Divine, considering the human-Divine connaturality. Dreams that were received on this topic are numerous. Below we quote a small number of them, all of which are verbatim and in English.

- *I am that I am.*
- *I need a referent, and that is my referent.*
- *That is everything together.*
- *I am one also many.*
- *That is my whole I.D.*
- *That is the secret of my being.*
- *All that there is is the foot of my being.*
- *Whole I is my double you.*
- *The world is my external half.*
- *My internal half is extended in space and time.*
- *I am one; made up of two.*
- *All "I" is two there.*
- *My subjective side is one; my objective side is two.*
- *My inner half is all that.*
- *The external half of mine is dead.*

In chapter 7, the deity of the self is vindicated. If I am an entity that at every moment becomes what I see and if that which I see is the Divine, then I am divinized simply on the strength of my ability to see. Our dreams specify that all of us are God as we are since that which is there is God and happens to us spontaneously as breathing does. However, to acquire a divinized selfhood, we have to become aware of having such a status. Thus the important condition for our divinization is the knowledge that what we see or think is the Divine. In other words, seeing the Divine in everything makes us Divine. Some dreams that are specific about this topic are cited below:

- *You mean I when you say I.*
- *Man is God.*
- *He who sees, sees God; hence he is God.*
- *Do you understand that your company is always the Divine?*
- *See the object you look at as God.*
- *Identity (the self) of all is God.*
- *He is right on the other side.*
- *If we live with Him (fill our minds with them), He lives with us.*
- *Seeing a tree (for example) is equal to seeing God.*

The doctrine that the self is divine poses some serious questions. Chapter 8 considers these questions and aims at finding an answer for each of them based on the dicta of the received dreams. When the dreams say "Man is God," this can mean both are identical or it can mean there is only man in the world and God is another name for man. Also, if God is the whole, does that not leave the human self as a mere name? Our dreams pinpoint that God is the whole existence and men, in general, are parts of Him, but those, who attain the status of deity, are the ones who become fully cognizant of being parts or partners of God. Thus, the conclusion we have drawn from our dreams is that humans, in one sense, are non-entities if they think they are separate from God and derived their existence from their own nature; in another sense, each is all if they see themselves as parts and partners of the Divine. Here are some dreams that substantiate what was stated above:

- *God is all, the self is part of all.*
- *You are parts and parcels of me.*
- *You are both in my subjective and objective side.*
- *Trying energy as part is waste.*
- *Total of "I" is expressed both in my internal and my external halves.*
- *My background is your background.*
- *My being forms your inner and outer halves.*

Chapter 9 expounds the implication and the role of the self as a part of the Divine. The fundamental questions often asked are: Why are we here? What is the purpose of life? What is at the end of the road? The received dreams make it clear that when we become convinced that we are part of the Divine, we also become, in a sense, His being and His partner. Specifically, we assume the role of a viceregent on earth. As His deputy, we carry out, on His behalf, tasks we think He wants to be done for the good of all. Our dreams also indicate that there is life after death for those who realize their status of selfhood or Godhood. The last statement is both important and relevant; otherwise, human existence, as a consumer, striver, sufferer or do-gooder, for a short term, becomes senseless and finds expression in what Longfellow said: "Fleeting as were the dreams of old, remembered like a tale that's told, we pass away." The dreams, referring to our role as viceregent, are innumerable, the ones quoted below are clear specimens of them:

- *You imagine yourself in my shoes.*
- *Through the consciousness of humans, I and the world will be known.*
- *Things worthwhile to me, share with other people.*
- *You need to decide whether you live for yourself or for God.*
- *(You need to ponder) what you are made of; what you are made for.*
- *The fellow who did not know himself demanded so much. The fellow who knew himself did not demand anything.*
- *All you have to do is to say what it is that He wants to happen (on earth).*
- *Do it in the way you believe He thinks it should be done.*
- *Do whatever you can.*

- *Then you will truly value being human.*
- *Then you become convinced about the future life.*

It should be added that the messages contained in the above short dreams, fully correspond with the messages of thousands of our long dreams when broken down and analyzed. If I am asked what I have learned from my 40 years of involvement with the study of over a hundred thousand dreams, in a word, my response would be: nearly all of us, without our own fault, do not know who we really are. The concept of self is extremely complicated. We acquired no knowledge about it since nobody taught us such knowledge. When we do not know who we are, we can hardly do anything right. In a way, we are like those who are under the spell of hypnosis. We say and do things, but we do not know what motivates us to do so. Once we realize our true self, not only will we come to know the Deity, but we also find that we are also part of Him. We experience God's power in ourselves at any junction and see Him present in whatever we do. We do not say "I" write, "I" teach, "I" invent, etc. We sense that it is God within us who does the writing, teaching, inventing and whatever proceeds from us. Adopting such an outlook is not illogical; as in truth all forces and energy in us are self-acting or spontaneous. We find nothing in our multifarious dynamic systems being self-made. Thus, it seems fitting to finish the topic with this poem from the Persian poet, Hafez:

> "See in your own face, the sample of the work of art of the Divine;
> You are given a mirror in which to see the artist who produced such designs."

It is hoped that the above assertions, in addition to the body of the book, provoke further investigation into the source and contents of dreaming. This author must admit that although, he has generally presented his findings with a high level of confidence based on the great number of dreams he has had, yet he must acknowledge that in some areas, he did not reach the mark of apodictic certainty. Hence, the desideratum in this arena would be for further in-depth research.

In conclusion, if I were asked to summarize very briefly the messages of received dreams about the genuine self, I would say that the dreams dwell on the fact that very few of us really know who we are. Since the concept of the genuine or deified self has been unknown, no one has had a chance to learn it. Specifically, the dreams declare: "What you think is your self is not yourself." Yet everyone is as sure about having a self as one is sure about possessing a body. However, such a presumptuous self, according to received dreams, is not genuine. It is illusory, separative, and undeified. Hence, it is the source of most personal and social problems.

The genuine self is unitive and deified. With such a perception of the self, at any instant of contact, we see the other not only as part of ourselves but also as part of the Divine. Moreover, we consider the other as the Creator of our conscious life and the Weaver of our memories. We become convinced that without the other our genuine self cannot be realized, and since the other is part of the all-encompassing Divine, we become divinized or deified simply through the act of seeing. If we understand we are not self-made, but whatever we have is given to us spontaneously by a source outside of ourselves, then we think of ourselves as being gods and solve human problems as God. Under the influence of our illusory self, one sees oneself as an island unto itself. Therefore, self-centeredness , unrelatedness, superficiality, and hollowness characterize us. We become not only insular but insolent.

Today some with overweening hubris and some with great amazement speak of the boons of the phenomenal developments achieved in various fields of science and technology, but these developments have brought their banes also. The invention of better means of communication and extraordinary forces of mass destruction have also provided more diabolical tools for exploitation, control, corruption, violence, subjugation, destruction, aggression, and war. Thus the question is: Are we today safer, more content, more balanced, or more godlike than the ancients? If not, our dreams remind us that our pains and problems result from the illusory concept we have of the self or from the fact that we have more and more disidentified with our deified self. As long as this is not understood, the downfall trend in which at present almost the entire civilized world is caught, will remain unchanged, or it may even be accelerated.

Notes

Chapter 2

1. Quoted in Rogers, 267-268.
2. Quoted in Peters, 545.
3. Quoted in Frondizi, 115-116.
4. See Buber, 93.
5. Quoted in Jersild, 9.
6. Ibid. 10.
7. Ibid. 18.
8. See Hall & Lindzey, 476.
9. See Jaynes, 23.
10. Quoted in Brightman, 185.
11. Quoted in Jaynes, 2.
12. Quoted in Goswami, 208.
13. Ibid. 270.
14. Quoted in Rogers, 244.
15. Quoted in Rogers, 309.
16. Quoted in Naese, 287.
17. Quoted in Herbert, 250.
18. See Capra (1984), 252.
19. See *The Upanishads*, 77.
20. Quoted in Randal & Buchler, 363.

Chapter 3

1. Quoted in Herbert, 72.
2. See Domash in *World Government News,* 18.

3. See Capra (1984), 295.
4. See Wigner, 172.
5. Quoted in Russell, 44-45.
6. Ibid. 794.
7. Quoted in Peter, 477.
8. Quoted in Russell, 736.

Chapter 4

1. Quoted in Russell, 797.
2. Quoted in Naese, 52.
3. Quoted in Peters, 46.
4. See Watts (1968), 144.
5. See Watts (1963), 76.
6. See Watts (1968), 116.
7. Quoted in Norris, 80.
8. Quoted in Wright, 441.
9. Quoted in Herbert, 282.
10. See Alcott in *Treasure of Philosophy,* 23.
11. Quoted in Capra (1984), 282.
12. Quoted in Russell, 405.

Chapter 5

1. See Hocking, 18-19.
2. See Kuspit, 211.
3. See O'Dea, 34.
4. See Davis, 200.
5. See Brightman, 237.
6. See Merton, 34.
7. Quoted in Randal & Buchler, 283.
8. Quoted in Russell, ???
9. See Sperling, 21.

Chapter 6

1. See McDormott, 63.

2. See Emmet, 139.

Chapter 7

1. See Watts (1966), 81.
2. Ibid., 9.
3. Quoted in Rogers, 178.
4. Quoted in Russell, 405.
5. Quoted in Randal & Buchler, 279.
6. See Nicholson, *Silent Encounter,* 119.
7. See Wright, 501.
8. See Schrodinger, 95.

Chapter 8

1. See Clark, 177
2. Quoted in Rogers, 208.
3. See Nicholson, 257.
4. Ibid., 255.
5. Quoted in Huxley, 175.
6. See Malebranche, 780.
7. See Ludwig, 73.
8. See Huxley, 98.
9. See Watts (1971), 187.
10. Quoted in Rogers, 145.
11. See Wolfson, 165.
12. See Beckwith, 9.
13. See Titus, 231.
14. See Russell, 48.
15. See Huxley, 5.
16. See Pribram, "Psychology Today," Feb. 1979.
17. See Rogers, 231.
18. See Capra, 282.

Chapter 9

1. See Dupre, 258.

2. See Bakhtiar, 12. "Human beings" added for clarification.
3. See Zohar, 47.
4. See Ludwig, 63.
5. See Russell, 644.
6. See Peters, 268.
7. See Rogers, 314.
8. See Buber, 105.
9. See Schmitt, 98.
10. See Shah, 292.

Bibliography

Alcott, Amos Bronson. *Table Talk*. In Dagobert D., ed., *A Treasure of Philosophy*. New York: Grolier, 1995.

Bakhtiar, Laleh. *Sufi: Expressions of the Mystic Quest*. New York: Thames and Hudson Inc., 1987.

Brightman, E.S. *An Introduction to Philosophy*. New York: Henry Holt and Company, 1925.

Buber, M. *I and Thou*. New York: Charles Scribner's Sons, 1958.

Capra, F. *The Tao of Physics*. New York: Bantam Books, 1984.

Clark, Mary. "Plotinus." in Paul Edwards, ed., *The Encyclopedia of Philosophy*. London: Collie-Macmillan, 1967.

Davies, Paul. *The Mind of God: The Scientific Basis for a Rational World*. New York: Simon and Schuster, 1986.

Domash, L.H. "The Physics of Unity." in *World Government News*. Oct 1978. Pg 18.

Dupre, Louis. "Mysticism." in M. Eliado, ed. *The Encyclopedia of Religion*. New York: Macmillan, 1986.

Edwards, T. *The New Dictionary of Quotations*. London: Waverly Book Co., 1934.

Emmet, Dorothy. "Whitehead and Alexander." in *Process Studies*. vol. 21, no. 3, Fall 1992.

Frondizi, Risieri. *The Nature of the Self.* New Haven: Yale University Press, 1953.

Goswami, Amit. *The Self-Aware Universe.* New York: Tarcher/Putnam, 1993.

Hall, Calvin & Lindzey, G. *Theories of Personality.* New York: John Wiley, 1967.

Hepburn, Ronal W. "Mysticism, Nature and Assessment of." in Paul Edwards, ed. *The Encyclopedia of Philosophy.* London: Collier-Macmillan, 1967.

Herbert, Nick. *Elemental Mind: Human Consciousness and New Physics.* New York: Plume/Penguin, 1994.

Huxley, Aldous. *The Perennial Philosophy.* New York: Harper Colophon Books, 1970.

Jaynes, J. *The Origin of Consciousness in the Breakdown of the Bicameral Mind.* Boston: Houghton Mifflin, 1976.

Jersild, Arthur T. *In Search of the Self.* New York: Teacher's College, Columbia University, 1952.

Kuspit, Donald. *Whitehead's God and Metaphysics.* Pennsylvania State University Press, 1962.

Lang, R.D. *Self and Others.* Tavistock Publications Limited, 1961.

Malebranche, Nicolas. in Dagobert, D., ed., *A Treasure of Philosophy,* 1955.

Merton, Thomas. *The New Man*. New York: Farrar, Straus & Giroux, 1980.

Naess, Arne. *Four Modern Philosophers*. Chicago: The University of Chicago Press, 1965.

Nicholson, Wm. M. "Jung's Concept of the Self and Inner Experience." in Virginia Hanson ed.,

Silent Encounter: Reflection on Mysticism. Wheaton, Illinois: The Theosophical Publishing House, 1974.

Norris, Richard A. "Ontology." in M. Eliade, ed., *Encyclopedia of Religion*. New York: Macmillan, 1986.

O'Dea, Thomas F. *The Sociology of Religion*. Englewood Cliffs, New Jersey: Prentice-Hall, 1966.

Peters, R.S. ed., *Brett's History of Psychology*. Cambridge, Massachusetts: The M.I.T. Press, 1965.

Pribram, Carl. in *Psychology Today*. Feb. 1979.

Randal, J.H. & Buchler, J. *Philosophy: An Introduction*. New York: Barnes & Noble, 1952.

Rogers, Arthur K. *A Student History of Philosophy*. New York: Macmillan, 1923.

Rogers, C.R. *Client-Centered Therapy: Its Current Practice, Implications, and Theory*. New York: Hinds, 1948.

Russell, Bertrand. *A History of Western Philosophy*. New York: Simon and Shuster, 1945.

Schmitt, Richard. "Husserl, Edmund." in Paul Edwards ed., *Encyclopedia of Philosophy*. London: Macmillan, 1967.

Schroedinger, E. *My View of the World*. C. Hastings, trans. Woodbridge, Conneticut: Oxbow Press, 1983.

Shah, I. *The Sufis*. Garden City, New York: Anchor Books, 1971.

Smith, Huston. *The Religions of Man*. New York: Harper and Row, 1965.

Sperling, S. David. "God: In Post-Biblical Christianity." in M. Eliade, ed. *Encyclopedia of Religion*. New York: Macmillan, 1986.

Titus, Harold H. *Living Issues in Philosophy*. New York: American Book Co., 1959.

The Upanishads. The principal texts selected and translated from the original Sanskit by Prabahavanada and Frederick Manchester. New York: A Mentor Book, 1946.

Watts, Alan. *The Way of Zen*. New York: Vantage Books, 1957.

Watts, Alan. *The Supreme Identity: An Essay on Oriental Metaphysics and the Christian Religion*. New York: Vintage Books, 1972.

Watts, Alan W. *The Book: On the Taboo Against Knowing Who You Are*. New York: Collier Books, 1968.

Watts, Alan W. *Cloud-Hidden: Whereabouts Unknown*. New York: Vintage Books, 1974.

Watts, Alan W. *Psychotherapy: East and West*. New York: A Mentor Book, 1963.

Wigner, Eugene P. *Symmetries and Reflections: Scientific Essays*. Bloomington, Indiana: Indiana University Press, 1967.

Wolfson, H.A. *The Philosophy of Spinoza: Volume 1*. New York: Schocken Books, 1969.

Wright, W.K. *A History of Modern Philosophy*. New York: Macmillan, 1964.

Zohar, Danah. *The Quantum Self.* New York: William Morrow & Co., 1990.

Index